StreetWays

StreetWays

Chronicling the Homeless in Miami

EDITED BY

Eugene F. Provenzo, Jr.
Edward Ameen
Alain Bengochea
Kristen Doorn
Ryan W. Pontier
Sabrina F. Sembiante

PHOTOGRAPHS BY

Lewis Wilkinson

A Collaborative Project of the Dunspaugh-Dalton Community and Educational
Well-Being Research Center and Information Age Publishing

UNIVERSITY OF MIAMI
SCHOOL of EDUCATION
& HUMAN DEVELOPMENT

U

≡*IAP*

INFORMATION AGE PUBLISHING, INC.
Charlotte, NC • www.infoagepub.com

Library of Congress Cataloging-in-Publication Data

A CIP record for this book is available from the Library of Congress
http://www.loc.gov

ISBN: 978-1-62396-756-7 (Paperback)
       978-1-62396-757-4 (Hardcover)
       978-1-62396-758-1 (ebook)

Cover design by Theresa Bramblett, using photographs by Lewis Wilkinson.

Printed in the United States of America

Dedicated to Roberta Ann Olson

Bobbie asked that we "Please Acknowledge" homeless people.
A short video can be accessed online at: http://vimeo.com/28966247

Contents

Interviewees

Foreword

Street Ways is the second book in the University of Miami School of Education and Human Development Series with Information Age Publishing (IAP). The book series aims to bring to the public innovative approaches and tools for wellness promotion in diverse communities. Street Ways was created by students and faculty in the SOEHD concerned both about homelessness in our communities and by the general apathy and disconnection with which so many of us respond to homeless people. We are excited by this collaboration with IAP and the possibilities it affords both the research community and the general public.

Etiony Aldarondo, Ph.D.
Associate Dean for Research
Director, Dunspaugh-Dalton Community
& Educational Well-Being (CEW) Research Center
School of Education and Human Development
Executive Director, Council on Contemporary Families

Preface

The project described in this book, *StreetWays*, began as a result of a chance meeting between Eugene F. Provenzo, Jr., a professor at the University of Miami, and Lewis Wilkinson, a former business executive and documentary photographer. Lewis had been working through his church for some time in downtown Miami, helping homeless and street people access food and shelter, as well as medical care. In the process, he began to document their lives by taking photographs of them. Convinced that street people deserved to be better understood as individuals by the larger Miami community, he developed the idea of doing postcard or trading card-sized portraits of individuals, which would include not only the picture of a person but a brief biography of who they were. Lewis's idea was to provide street people (who are largely anonymous to the larger community) with an identity they could share with others— who they are, and their hopes and needs.

StreetWays is unique in that it goes beyond simply recording the lives of people on the street, to providing them with a means of describing who they are and what they care about that they can share with others including friends, family acquaintances, social workers and the general public. By providing homeless individuals postcards or trading cards to share, Lewis felt that they would be able to make a connection to the larger community and overcome something of their anonymity.

Following several discussions with Lewis about his work, Gene Provenzo proposed that it might be interesting to have a group of his doctoral students at the University of Miami engage in the collection of interviews with his photographic subjects and to develop a series of projects including an exhibit, a photo-documentary book and a website that would feature their stories. He conceived the project as an experiment in community visual and social literacy, as well as community well-being.

After a careful review by the university, the project was formally launched in late March 2010. A total of twenty-eight homeless individuals were eventually identified who wished to be interviewed and photographed. In addition, key homeless advocates and support people in the community provided background on the conditions and needs of Miami's homeless population. Interviews were conducted at the First United Methodist Church in downtown Miami, and on the street in downtown Miami and Miami Beach during March and April 2010.

* * *

We would like to acknowledge the help of Associate Dean Etiony Aldorando whose support and encouragement was invaluable in helping us make this project happen. Thanks go to Dean Isaac Prilleltensky whose vision about the need for community-based studies inspired much of this work. Dr. Cynthia Weems and her staff at the First United Methodist Church of Miami provided invaluable resources and assisance. Stefano Campanini from the Etra Fine Art Gallery in the Wynwood District provided us important encouragement and support in the first phases of this project.

Thanks finally go to Patricia Thorp for her encouragement, and Asterie B. Provenzo for her continuing support and editing.

Eugene F. Provenzo, Jr.
Lewis Wilkinson
Edward Ameen
Alain Bengochea
Kristen Doorn
Ryan W. Pontier
Sabrina F. Sembiante

May 2010

INTRODUCTION

Homelessness currently exists as one of the primary, and most misinterpreted, social problems in the United States (National Alliance to End Homelessness, 2007). While many view the phenomenon of homelessness as a permanent condition, this is not necessarily the case. Poverty-induced homelessness is often a temporary condition. Homelessness, due to mental issues or drug-related problems, is often more long-lasting (Drake, Osher, and Wallach, 1999). In addition, there are those who voluntarily choose to live on the streets.

Accurately measuring homelessness is a difficult task. The experience of homelessness for individuals is not fixed, but rather changes over time due to a wide-range of variables. Each individual's homeless experience is different according to the individual's age, gender, family background, psychological state, and social support, as well as the general condition of the local and national economy (National Coalition for the Homeless: How Many People Experience Homelessness, 2009).

In 2000, 2.3 to 3.5 million individuals of those identified as living in poverty in the United States experienced some extended period of homelessness (The Urban Institute, 2000). With the recent decline in the economy, homeless populations are on the rise (Foreclosure to Homelessness, 2009).

While various sources of assistance and support exist for homeless people, not everyone receives help, and the demand for services frequently exceeds capacity. A recent survey of 23 cities showed that 12 are unable to provide sufficient shelter spaces to people in need (U.S. Conference of Mayors, 2007). Moreover, shelters in rural areas of the United States are often not available (Brown, 2002), despite the fact that 9% of the homeless U.S. population is situated outside of urban and suburban areas (The Council for Affordable and Rural Housing, n.d.).

For those who are able to secure refuge in emergency shelters, average lengths of stay are 69 days for single men, 51 days for single women, and 70 days for families. Comparatively, increases in average length of stay have been reported in transitional housing, with single men, single women, and families staying 175, 196, and 223 days, respectively. The longest lengths of stay in shelters were recorded at permanent supportive housing locations, where the average stay was 556 days for single men, 571 days for single women, and 604 days for families (U.S. Conference of Mayors, 2008).

Homelessness is a phenomenon that affects both individuals and family units, and people of all ages, races, and socio-economic levels. It exists throughout the country (National Alliance to End Homelessness, 2007). Although people living in poverty are at the greatest risk of experiencing homelessness, variables such as declining wages, the poor economy, and unaffordable housing can affect persons from all income levels by increasing one's chances of becoming homeless (National Coalition for the Homeless: Who is Homeless, 2009; National Coalition for the Homeless: Why are People Homeless?, 2009).

According to statistics from The National Law Center on Homelessness and Poverty (2004), 39% of homeless people are children aged 18 or under, with 42% of those children aged five and under. Many of these minors (5% of the homeless population) were found to be unaccompanied. Persons between the ages of 25 and 34 make up 25% of the U.S. homeless population, while persons between the ages of 55 and 64 account for 6% of the population (The National Law Center on Homelessness and Poverty, 2004). Geographic location accounts for a large influence in the representation of race in homelessness statistics. An overrepresentation of Whites, Native Americans, and migrant workers is commonly found in rural areas (U.S. Department of Agriculture, 1996) and an overrepresentation of African-Americans and Hispanics are commonly found in metropolitan city shelters (U.S. Conference of Mayors, 2006).

Much of the public's misunderstanding of homelessness stems from ignorance of the factors that combine together to create the situation of being homeless. While a shortage of affordable rental housing and an increase in poverty are major factors contributing to homelessness for adults and families, there are other direct and indirect causes that contribute to the problem as well. The recent economic recession, causing the loss of jobs and income, has made it impossible for many people to meet mortgage and rent payments, which in turn leads to the risk of foreclosure, eviction, and subsequent poverty and/or homelessness.

Poverty and homelessness have also increased due to a decline in public support programs and the fact that several cash-assistance programs have been replaced with block-grant programs because these sources of assistance do not keep up with inflation. Other factors include lack of affordable health care, domestic violence, abuse, mental illness, and addiction disorders (National Coalition for the Homeless, 2009).

In Florida, the number one cited reason for homelessness is unemployment or underemployment, followed by medical and disability issues (28% of the homeless report physical disabilities, 28% report mental illness, and 35% report drug and alcohol addictions). Housing issues rank as the third largest contributor to homelessness, followed by family issues, removal from one's current home, recent immigration status, and then natural or other disasters (Florida Department of Children and Families, 2009). In 2009, 50% of people identified as homeless in the state were encountering their first experience of homelessness, while 39% had been experiencing homelessness for more than one year. 15% of the homeless people in Florida were U.S. military veterans and 18% were married (Ibid).

Among the characteristics of homelessness, and the difficulties that follow, is that homeless people often lose their sense of self worth, self-efficacy, and psychosocial identity (Buckner, Bassuk, & Sima, 1993 as seen in Boydell, Goering, & Morrell-Bellai, 2000). Added to this lack of self-identity are the stereotypes that prevail in society of homeless people, which include stigmas such as laziness, disempowerment, and passivity—values that are inconsistent with American traditions of competitiveness, self-reliance, and personal achievement (Cohen & Wagner, 1992, as seen in Boydell, Goering, & Morrell-Bellai, 2000).

Miami-Dade County's Community Homeless Plan

The most recent statistics for homelessness in Miami reflect that as of January 2010, there were 3,832 homeless people in Miami-Dade County, 759 of whom lived on the streets and 3,073 of whom lived in emergency shelters, transitional housing, or motels (Miami-Dade Homeless Trust, 2010). Of those homeless individuals who reside on the streets, 67% stay within the City of Miami limits, 20% stay on Miami Beach, 9% stay in the unincorporated southern part of the county, and 4% stay in the unincorporated northern part of the county (Ibid). Forty-four percent of street-dependent people were counted as African-American, 15% as white, 30% as Hispanic, and another 12% were not identified by their ethnicity (Ibid). Based on our experience working on this project, these figures are almost certainly very low when compared to the actual numbers of homeless individuals who seem to be on the street. The census count was conducted during an unusually cold day in Miami and reflects a reduction of nearly 500 homeless people from one year earlier.

In July 1993, the Board of County Commissioners in Miami-Dade County adopted a continuum of care plan known as the "Miami-Dade County Community Homeless Plan." This plan was developed in order to initiate a comprehensive strategy for both the implementation and coordination of housing and services for homeless residents of Miami through a continuum of care (Miami-Dade County, 2010). It includes a variety of preventative measures that are to be implemented as a part of the plan's 10-year initiative to end homelessness. These measures include the implementation of the following services: prevention and diversion programs, outreach teams according to geography, supportive services, permanent supportive housing, transitional housing and treatment, and HAC emergency shelters (Miami-Dade County Homeless Trust, 2008).

Along with the adoption of the Community Homeless Plan, the Board of County Commissioners also approved the levying of a one-cent food and beverage tax, which would provide a dedicated source of income and funding for homeless programs. As a result of these efforts, the Miami-Dade County Homeless Trust was implemented. The trust carries out the policy initiatives developed by the Trust Board. It also assists in monitoring contract compliance by agencies who work closely with Miami-Dade County, through the trust, to provide housing and other services for homeless individuals. Funding for the trust comes from food and beverage proceeds as well as the U.S. Department of Housing and Urban Development and the State of Florida. The Homeless Trust also partners with and receives support from the Community Partnership for the Homeless (CPH), a non-profit organization that runs and manages two Homeless Assistance Centers—The Chapman Center in downtown Miami and the South Miami-Dade Center in Homestead. In 1998, the Homeless Trust was honored for being a "National Model" and showing "Best Practice" for addressing homelessness (Miami Dade County, 2010).

The Homeless in Miami: Perceptions of Service Providers

I think it's important that people don't forget that we are here to service people in need, and we have to be flexible in meeting their needs.

-Ben Burton, Miami Coalition for the Homeless

Support from governmental organizations and charities are essential to the survival of unsheltered people in Miami. Without assistance, these individuals would almost certainly find themselves unable to meet their basic needs. Often such assistance can be the difference between life and death.

As part of our research, we conducted a number of interviews with various individuals serving homeless populations in Miami. These interviews were conducted primarily by a member of our research team, Edward Ameen, an experienced homeless advocate who has worked as the Miami Executive Director of *StandUp For Kids*, a national non-profit organization that helps homeless teens and young adults through street outreach, mentoring, and prevention programs.

Dr. Cynthia Weems

Dr. Cynthia Weems is one of the many individuals interviewed for this project who is involved in providing services for homeless individuals in the Miami community. She is a pastor at the First United Methodist Church in downtown Miami. For approximately thirty years the church has had a regular program providing valuable services for homeless individuals living in shelters and on the streets—most notably serving breakfast three days a week for the past twenty years. Cynthia sees many people showing up at the church who have become homeless gradually. She explains,

> Some have stories where they have burned every bridge, and every cousin and every sibling, and nobody else is taking them in. Sometimes there seems to be less of that and more of "I tried to make it on my own, my girlfriend kicked me out; my roommate didn't work out, and now I don't have any money." In a place like Miami, there's a big gap between having a bed and not having a bed. You can't just go and rent a room very easily. Especially with the climate, one week turns into three months.[1]

---

1   Interview with Cynthia Weems conducted by Eugene F. Provenzo, Jr. and Lewis

Cynthia sees the homeless population in Miami facing problems at multiple levels. "There are mental health issues. There are health issues. Their teeth are falling out. They have ulcers. Some have AIDS."[2] She feels that systemic problems, including drug addiction, unemployment, and hunger, need to be addressed. She also recognizes that there is a certain number of people who, for whatever reason, simply prefer to live on the street.

Cynthia feels the process of getting the homeless back into the workforce is complex. Many homeless individuals are apprehensive about succeeding. Others have unrealistic expectations about how much their work is worth. As a result, they choose street life instead.

Having come to Miami from the Midwest, Cynthia feels that Miami is more tolerant and provides more services for homeless populations than other places where she has worked. Still, she feels that these efforts are inadequate and represent a "band-aid" on a much larger social problem, which can only be addressed through systemically and carefully implemented change.

Earnie Earth

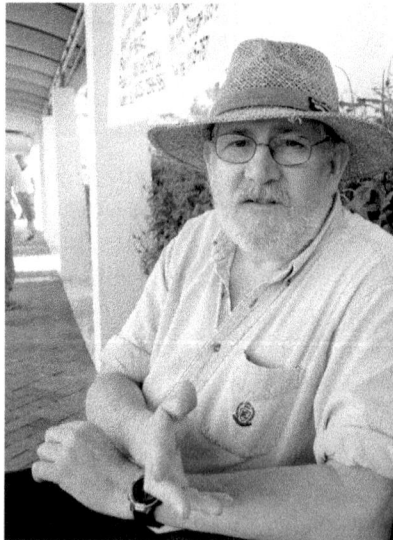

Ernie Earth works with HOPE in Miami Beach, a faith-based program whose main method of outreach is a bi-monthly program that provides homeless individuals with food, clothing, shoes, pre-

Porter Wilkinson, March 8, 2010, Miami, Florida.
2   Ibid.

scription eye glasses, hygiene products, nutritional products, haircuts, first aid, and HIV testing. These meetings are held at the Miami Beach Community Church in the center of the Lincoln Road tourist district. Ernie's role in this group is to help homeless clients obtain birth certificates, state identification cards, and Social Security cards.

> We buy people Florida I.D.s. If they had one, I order it online. If they haven't had one, we order them a birth certificate.... And then we have an agreement with the City of Miami Beach. They call the Department of Motor Vehicles and they get the first five appointments every Monday, and with our money they buy them Florida I.D.s.[3]

HOPE's identification program is particularly important because without identification, it is almost impossible for people to obtain regular work.

Ernie was homeless himself for a number of years. He dealt drugs and had an alcohol problem that prevented him from being able to afford his rent. He sees himself as now doing "socially relevant work." Commenting on his own unwillingness to stop using drugs or to stop drinking and get help, he says,

> I wasted oxygen by breathing. . . . It was always about me. Today, I live to help others—I earn the air... I'm useful. I never would have dreamed that I would have a useful, fulfilling life.

He says that the general public is upset with homeless individuals, because:

> They don't like seeing the people sleeping in the doorways, people using the bathroom in the doorways, and we're helping stop this. . . . There are some people you cannot help. They want to bum a beer, steal a car radio at 2:00 in the morning. They don't want to be under no rules, no restrictions. But most people realize that the apparent freedom of being homeless comes at a great price . . . The homeless have to make an effort to change their situation and not just be dependent on others acting for them. . . . If you want to work, you need to be clean. People can't let themselves smell and expect to get work. . . . They can have hope. They have to decide that they want to get off the streets, and do what it takes. . . .[4]

---

3   Interview with Ernie Earth conducted by Edward Ameen, April 10, 2010, Miami Beach, Florida.
4   Ibid.

Ernie doesn't expect people to change without any help. "They need a counselor, they need someone to talk to, someone to encourage them."[5] In the end though, Ernie explains that people have to take responsibility for their own lives.

Mary Andrews

Mary Andrews is the Executive Director of Miami Bridge Youth and Family Services, which is primarily an emergency shelter for displaced and runaway teens. Her organization provides approximately 40 beds for youths under the age of 18 who are in need. From Mary's vantage point, one which has been shaped by a lifelong residency in Florida and a father who was involved in local politics, she believes a great deal more can be done to prevent these youth from becoming homeless and disconnected members of the community as they move into adulthood.

Many of the youth the Miami Bridge serves are in foster care and are wards of the state. Under the current system, a mandate offers youth who are aging out of foster care a stipend called "Road to Independence," which can, however, put them on a road to homelessness.

It is not good to take someone who has never lived alone before and say "Okay, you're 18 now. Here's your thousand dollars. You're going to go to school. We'll find a little efficiency apartment and give you this fur-

---

5   Ibid.

niture here. As long as you are in school, you're going to get this check for the next year.[6]

Another policy that does not work in practice is the notion that all youth who run away need to be reunifited with their families. The reality is that many of the young people Mary serves have no experience with stable family conditions and a large percentage find themselves in families who cannot, or do not wish to, take care of their children.

> Many people have the notion that the best thing is for these people to be with a family. And a big piece of that is probably true, if in fact there was a perfect world and a perfect family.[7]

Living instead in a group or residential setting may be the closest sub-stitute for an actual family that these young people will have, while they learn the benefits and responsibilities of being a part of a community. The problem is, however, that Miami has extremely limited options for at-risk and homeless youth in need of housing.

Mary strives for the Miami Bridge to be a "center of excellence" in emergency care, which is difficult given the varied histories of youth who enter at all times of the day. There are, however, some common successful practices.

> What works is structure, no holds barred. I think you have to have high expectations. . . . You have to commend them for even living to the age that they are. There is something in their souls, hearts, or minds that said to them that they are worth living. There is something and we have to identify what that is. But you cannot identify that in brief intervals; it just does not happen.[8]

The challenge in preparing youth who are in "survival mode" to be-come flourishing adults resides in providing better care to more youth in need. Mary chides, "Services need to be expedited. I am on a lot of dart boards because I keep hounding everybody."

Homeless youth who are in places like the Miami Bridge have at least a few advocates in their corner. Though they need help desperately, many youth do not make it to the shelters. One solution, according to Mary, is a better network of care.

---

6   Interview with Mary Andrews conducted by Edward Ameen, April 12, 2010, Miami, Florida.
7   Ibid.
8   Ibid.

I think that we have to connect the dots. We have a lot of injection into the system, but we don't have a continuum. That is a shame. I believe that the money is there. . . . You have a lot of fiscal management in government, but you don't have a lot of service management looking at how effectively that money is being spent.[9]

The challenge in creating this network is "getting the people to believe they can work together."[10] This involves public and private agencies meeting the needs of youth at all points in a homeless continuum, from prevention, to intervention, to aftercare. So what has kept Miami from doing more for a very vulnerable population? According to Mary,

Florida is behind other states. I don't think that is because we have such a transient society. I think that Florida is simply not invested in caring for the vulnerable populations that we have as well as other states are. . . . Someone really needs to pick the torch up and step outside the box for Florida to change. I don't see that right now. We have to raise our expectations.[11]

Benjamin Burton

The sentiment that the state and county can do more for the homeless is echoed by Benjamin Burton, Executive Director of the Miami Coalition for the Homeless, an organization whose purpose is "to draw funding and political will around making sure people who are poor or homeless

---

9   Ibid.
10   Ibid.
11   Ibid.

get what they need." [12] He adds, "We are really about systems change, and collaborating at the state and federal levels to make sure those changes actually happen."[13] When asked to speak about some of the limitations for local homeless people, he reasoned that they are victims of a treatment system that harbors antiquated views of who is homeless and what their needs are:

> The treatment system hasn't evolved to develop around people who have service resistant problems and who have needs that the older, traditional system does not meet. You'll hear "housing first" and everyone will say that's a great idea. It's not a bad model but not a model for everyone, particularly if you've been homeless with chronic problems and you really need some transitional housing . . . some skill-building time, some time to makes some mistakes in a supportive environment. . . . The models we have right now are great if you are situationally homeless. But these models are high-demand; you have to be ready to engage in them.[14]

Extending services to the people who are "service resistant" and chronically homeless would seemingly impact many of the people whose stories appear in this book.

Who, then, become homeless in Miami? Although it's relatively easy to become homeless ("the number one reason is because people don't have any money"[15]), it is difficult to find one's way out of homelessness.

> The simplest of things you need—money, a living-wage job—are not going to come to fruition automatically. You can work full-time and still not have enough money to get an apartment and pay your bills. This is one of those twists that I think it's important that people need to understand. It's not that people who are homeless and poor aren't trying.[16]

If we know how people become and stay homeless, what keeps us from implementing the changes necessary to alleviate the burden of homelessness? For Ben, the problem is related to both misconceptions and prejudices. According to him, the conception of welfare mothers driving a Cadillac is a myth, just as people choosing homelessness as a lifestyle is a myth. It's also a myth that a person who is panhandling does so by

---

12   Interview with Benjamin Burton conducted by Edward Ameen, April 12, 2010, Miami, Florida.
13   Ibid.
14   Ibid.
15   Ibid.
16   Ibid.

choice. "When people do not have the systemic choices or supports [such as living-wage jobs and affordable housing] . . . then you're going to see them asking for things in places where they may be likely [to] receive some assistance."[17]

Ben is passionate about social justice and moved from clinical mental health into advocacy work because he saw so many individuals needing the same basic things. Central to the Coalition's mission is Ben's view that housing and healthcare are rights, things that a modern society should embrace.

Running contrary to this ideal are a set of prejudices that have direct effects on our treatment of the homeless and subsets of the homeless population—"the dirty secrets that people do not talk about."[18] Ben rattles these off clearly, which may be a sign that he encounters them often in his job. Broadly, he reasons that

> There are still a lot of value judgments about who is homeless and how they became homeless . . . People have different opinions about resources and who they should be allocated to.[19]

In specific ways, several groups of people are affected. Single men face the challenge that they are "somehow less worthy of services than a woman with children"[20] and consequently receive fewer and slower services. Sex offenders have been "legislated into homelessness" due to residency restrictions enforced—and later loosened—by municipalities such as Miami-Dade County, which got rid of "a buffer zone where people could live. That's why people live under the bridge."[21] People who are not disabled have fewer places to turn. "If you don't have a disability, the system doesn't really work for you."[22] According to Ben, immigrants are at a particular disadvantage. "You're not eligible for all the services you need to become self-sufficient and the system is not really in place to allow you to become a citizen so you can do that."[23] Race matters as well, "We have a high percentage of minorities in this city, and the racial tensions haven't been completely worked out." In a nutshell, "the darker you are, the poorer you are."[24]

---

17   Ibid.
18   Ibid.
19   Ibid.
20   Ibid.
21   Ibid.
22   Ibid.
23   Ibid.
24   Ibid.

Despite the work that needs to be done, Ben believes that Miami leads in ways that other major metropolitan areas do not,

> The city does have some unique things going on. We have a coalition that does pure advocacy, and we have a $6 million endowment. Most cities don't have that. We tax ourselves. Most places don't tax themselves to benefit poor people. We have a Homeless Trust that has been very successful in that model in drawing down dollars. We have a private and public partnership . . . which is really good at serving people in an emergency housing situation in a really dignified way. And there are some individual partners that are really good at developing housing and understanding the technology behind services and development. A lot of places don't have all those things coming together. A lot of this puts us on the cutting edge and poises us for when money does become available.[25]

In moving forward, Ben offers several suggestions. As a start, we must strive for a more accurate count of the homeless. "The only data on homelessness in Miami is held by the Homeless Trust. I think the methodology is flawed... A lot of people are excluded from the count. For example, if you're doubled up or in an institutional setting, you're not counted."[26]

As advice to service providers, Ben states, "Partnerships are critical now. Particularly in times of limited resources, people [must] streamline their organizations and share resources and information."[27] He also warns that providers must remain current in their knowledge about homelessness and remember that their true mission is to help people. "I think a lot of organizations have gotten into perpetuating their organizations, instead of what they originally got into business to do."[28]

When we consider how we can best help the homeless, "we have to be real careful about protecting people so that they never fall into homelessness. As far as treatment models, prevention is much cheaper and more effective."[29] When prevention fails to catch everyone in a safety net, Ben asks us to remember that "to serve homelessness, we don't have to build new communities. The whole idea is to reintegrate people into existing communities." In implementation, this translates into scattered housing, a model whereby "you don't know how much rent [your neighbors are] paying . . . there's no stigma. I think ghettoizing people and building housing projects doesn't work for a lot of reasons."[30]

---

25 Ibid.
26 Ibid.
27 Ibid.
28 Ibid.
29 Ibid.
30 Ibid.

Nationwide, there were 218 known fatal attacks against homeless people between 1999 and 2007, which far exceeded the number of fatal acts reported in all other legally recognized hate-crime categories. Florida has been given the title of the "Meanest State," with more violent acts committed against the homeless here than in any other state. From 2005-2007, there were 111 reported violent acts on homeless people in Florida, occurring in at least 31 different municipalities.

Ari Porth

Ari Porth is a Florida State Representative for District 96, which covers the area just north of Miami-Dade County. He was first elected to the House in 2004. Ari authored 24 bills in the 2010 legislative session and co-sponsored numerous others. In matters of state policy, he has been a strong advocate of the homeless. This year, he introduced HB11, dubbed the Homeless Hate Crimes Bill, which provides protection to homeless people by giving tougher sentences to perpetrators who attack them because they are homeless. The bill moved through the House and Senate and was signed into law by Governor Charlie Crist. Ari states that HB11 "sends the message that the majority of people in public office think that that we need to be protecting our most vulnerable."[31]

The bill was inspired by a January 12, 2006, attack on a 45-year-old homeless man in Fort Lauderdale, Florida, named Norris Gaynor. Three teenagers beat the man to death with a baseball bat for no apparent reason. Videos of the beating circulated on the internet. In the years that

---

31   Interview with Ari Porth conducted by Edward Ameen, April 29, 2010, Miami, Florida.

followed, Maryland became the first state to enact a homeless hate crimes bill, using the disturbing video of Mr. Gaynor's killing as argument for the bill's necessity. Florida is now the second state to pass the bill. According to Ari,

> Fort Lauderdale was portrayed by newspapers all over the country and even internationally as a hateful place to be, if you happened to be homeless. I thought we needed to fix our image.[32]

According to Ari, getting the bill passed was no easy feat. The bill's concepts were introduced twice previously by Representative Priscilla Taylor,

> She worked hard and I was proud to cosponsor her efforts when she tried, but there were objections . . . There was a conservative group of legislators that were fundamentally opposed to hate crimes in general. It's not necessarily that they have a problem with homelessness being added, they just don't like hate crimes and they don't want to add to them. So we had to change that mindset.[33]

Ari's district secretary Dan Daley confirmed that the struggle to get the bill passed was really intense due to ideological opposition to the bill.

To its advantage, the bill had the strong backing of Broward Sheriff Al Lamberti. "He committed the full support of his office and that was good —showing that it wasn't a bill pushed by democrats but a bipartisan effort . . . This wasn't a bill that people support from one party or another."[34] The bill, however was not without its detractors. A representative from another district commented that homeless people were "bums" and went on to say that they do not pay taxes and do not vote.

> That to me suggested such a lack of understanding and a lack of compassion on the issues. It made me feel like that if people really think that, we did the right thing by filing this bill.[35]

Ari feels that it is a civic duty to represent the disenfranchised.

> There's not a strong lobby for the homeless like there are for big businesses. I am not doing this because I'm anticipating campaign contributions . . . This is an issue that I care about and I'm doing it because I

---

32 Ibid.
33 Ibid.
34 Ibid.
35 Ibid.

made a commitment when I first took office.[36]

In fact, Ari often cites a Humphrey Bogart quote as a mantra he aspires to live by in public office, that goes to the effect that a society has to be judged by how it treats people in the dawn of life, the twilight of life, and the shadows of life. Dan confirms that Ari is there for everybody no matter who you are.

Ari's strives to stay connected to the needs of everyone in his district, especially when he's in the Capitol.

> I think that the majority of our legislators have a good heart and want to do the right thing. They just need to be reminded by people from their communities...The power of re-election, the fact that your district has the ability to hire and fire you, is very powerful and motivating, and it needs to be used.[37]

Pat Cawley

Pat Cawley is the Clinical Director of Camillus House, a major service provider to the homeless in Miami for the past 15 years, housing over 1,000 people per night in their continuum of programs that range from emergency shelter, to transitional and supportive housing, to scattered apartments, healthcare services, and other programs. Pat came from Boston 13 years ago as a consultant hired to develop a residential drug

36   Ibid.
37   Ibid.

treatment program for Camillus House. "I say that I was seduced by both Miami and Camillus House. I came in January of 1997 and it was cold up in Boston."[38]

At that time, Camillus House was serving primarily men and "had a reputation of being pretty rough. . . . We had very few services for women —a shower program one or two days a week. But because of the facilities we were in and the history of Camillus, we really catered to men. Services have become increasingly co-ed, but she wishes the homeless provider community could still do more. "If you ask people on the street who need the most help, they will tell you the mentally-ill women do. They tell us, 'help the women.'"[39] Pat explains that Miami-Dade, like many other counties, underreports its numbers of homeless women because they hide so well. Women, according to her, are dependent on their partners, who are mostly male. They are oftern addicted to the same drug as their partner. Frequently, they are pimped out for the drug. Pat believes that you really have to be tough to survive as a homeless woman in Miami.

With over a dozen residential programs under its direction, Camillus House is perhaps best known for its Courtyard Program which provides mattresses, food, showers, meals, and case management in an enclosed outdoor area.

> It's similar to being out on the streets, so for people who can't stand being in an enclosed area, this is like a perfect solution. We even have a little alleyway in between the building and the pavilion, which we created as a street so people can be out on the street still within the confines of our property. There are some benches and people play checkers and dominoes and cards.[40]

Pat believes that the program is a success, as they originally expected to serve 30-40 individuals per night but oftentimes find themselves at capacity with 170. "It's really developed into a community. . . . unlike other shelters, we don't expect people to get up and leave at 6 o'clock in the morning. We want them to stay with us and participate in the day-center programs and activities."[41] One requirement that people must adhere to is the curfew, which used to be later. When it was at 11:00, people would go out to get one last high. So the Courtyard Program shortened it to 10:00. Pat cites public health concerns such as H1N1 as another reason to enforce curfew.

---

38 Interview with Pat Cawley conducted by Edward Ameen, Miami, FL, May 4, 2010.
39 Ibid.
40 Ibid.
41 Ibid.

Camillus charges fees to stay in the Courtyard, which is based on recurring income such as money from Social Security or the Veteran's Administration. Pat calculated that it costs the program $8-10 per night per client, working out to $140 each month. Several people we interviewed were unhappy about these charges. Pat responded to this criticism as follows:

> We instituted the same rules that we have for our housing program. If someone wanted to stay with us, they had to provide a client contribution. A lot of people left when we instituted that, but we really could not in good conscience say "OK, come live with us," knowing they are using, going out, getting high and coming back to us, totally crashing and getting into fights.[42]

Former and present clients of Camillus House, like other shelter programs, are not shy in offering their opinions of the services they receive. Pat understands that these reviews are bound to be mixed.

> I think it depends on which program the people are in. The clients who go through our treatment program and into our housing program, who are with us for from 18 months to three years, they credit Camillus with saving their lives. I think a lot of the clients out on the street who haven't come into the Courtyard Program are angry at Camillus because of this perception that Camillus has all these resources that we're hoarding from people. I think that changed over the years, but I am sure that is still out there. I know that some in the community see us as enabling—we [are] not that "pick-yourselves-up-by-the-bootstraps" kind of program.[43]

Pat sees Miami as doing a good job, in general, to prevent and intervene in situations of temporary homelessness due to economic reasons. In these instances, "homeless providers play very nicely together in this community."[44] The services needing the most improvement are those in mental health. "Those remaining [on the street] are persistently mentally ill and it is very difficult to get services . . . We have a community mental health system where people are waiting six weeks to two-months to get an appointment.[45] The result of this wait is an influx of people using emergency hospital care to get medication.

42 Ibid.
43 Ibid.
44 Ibid.
45 Ibid.

The street-dependent homeless population in Miami faces a variety of challenges which are reflected in many of the stories we have collected in this book. According to Pat, "maybe only 5% are out there homeless by choice."[46] Some pockets of homeless people include those with mental illnesses, drug dependencies, personality disorders, intellectual limitations, traumatic brain injuries, and other organic disorders. Another sub-population are immigrants who lack paperwork, who never paid into Social Security during years of working in informal job networks, and now find themselves at the age of retirement without any resources. Countering a commonly held stereotype, Pat explains,

> I think that the perception that homeless people are lazy is just not true. These are folks who have fallen out of our system. These are the folks that the mental-health system didn't work for, and probably the foster-care system didn't work for.[47]

At the same time, she refutes the idea that becoming homeless is simply about economics.

> What a lot of folks have is social capital—they have family and friends they can stay with. The chronically homeless...are a population that have no social capital. They came from poverty to begin with. The functional family members are just getting by and cannot or will not take in the addicted brother or the uncle. The immigrants that we see have no family here . . . they are supposed to be supporting the ones back home and they can't do that anymore.[48]

According to Pat, getting off the street is not so easy, particularly for the chronically homeless.

> In some ways, they become addicted to life on the street. There's the rush from that, the high . . . There is the draw of the streets. You can make your own hours . . . When you're not housed, there aren't a lot of responsibilities, except to yourself, to stay safe and to get what you need. When you're housed, you need to pay bills and get along with your neighbor.[49]

What complicates the issue is loss of identity that people experience when they move off the street. "They lose their identity as a homeless

---

46   Ibid.
47   Ibid.
48   Ibid.
49   Ibid.

person, which in some ways may be much more comfortable than somebody who is housed,"[50] explained Pat. One program that addresses this is a "weaning process" that allows people to spend time between their supportive housing and the streets they have known for so long.

Resources for the Homeless

Each year the federal government commits to providing funds to offset the poor living standards for the homeless who are exposed to the harshest conditions in the United States. In 2008, the U.S. government provided $2.43 billion to 11 major homeless programs, an 11% increase from the year before (National Alliance to End Homelessness, 2008). Among many of the federally financed projects, support was given for homelessness prevention, medical care, shelter, and the reintegration of people into mainstream society. Alongside governmental organizations, many charities engaged in fundraising and supplying basic necessities to homeless populations. These charities, which include local church groups, missions, and voluntary and non-profit organizations, fill the gap in terms of education, shelter, outreach, healthcare, advocacy, and other services not provided by federal programs.

Although many services are available to the homeless, the homeless themselves are often unaware of many of the types of assistance that they can draw on. Many are discouraged by bureaucratic procedures that they encounter or are skeptical that such help might actually exist.

Living on the streets, the homeless population is continuously exposed to unsanitary conditions and potential disease. Finding safe places to sleep, bathe, wash clothes, and use the bathroom is a constant challenge. Because of financial constraints, they also tend to neglect their health, falling prey to parasites and infections. Those individuals active in the sex trade are more prone to sexually transmitted diseases and infections. Contrary to popular belief, most only enter this trade as a means of survival. It is especially prevalent for young runaways, of which at 15-30% have been commercially sexually exploited or trafficked (National Alliance to End Homelessness, 2009).

Evidence of how the homeless community suffers from greater health problems than the general community is indicated by the higher prevalence of HIV/AIDS among them—a situation that can largely be attributed to a lack of medical care and education. As estimated by the National Alliance to End Homelessness, 6.4% of homeless people were HIV-positive in 2009 (Homeless Conditions in Florida, 2009), compared to 0.4%

---

50   Ibid.

of adults and adolescents in the general population (Centers for Disease Control and Prevention, 2008).

Various services have been established to counter epidemics among the homeless, including telephone hotlines, educational programs, and medical programs (at no cost) to reduce infection from HIV/AIDS and other sexually transmitted diseases. The Florida AIDS Hotline provides immediate access to information regarding prevention as well as counseling for those afflicted with the disease. In addition to serving as an educational resource, it aims to inform homeless individuals infected with HIV/AIDS about the treatment they can receive within the community, such as how to apply to Florida's AIDS Drug Assistance program (ADAP) (a plan waiving all drug costs for HIV treatment). The South Florida AIDS Network, the largest service network in Miami, refers homeless persons infected with HIV, on a case-by-case basis, to healthcare professionals. Their services include mental health therapy, prescription drugs, oral health care, eye care, nutritional services, substance abuse treatment programs, and transportation assistance.

Additional Resources for the Homeless Population in South Florida

Several public and private facilities receiving federal grants from the Department of Health and Human Services provide general medical care, prescription treatment, and transportation for those in need. This assistance granted by the Health Care for the Homeless program enables homeless individuals to visit Jackson Memorial Hospital, Community Health of South Florida, Florida Health Centers of Southwest Florida, and Camillus House for any primary medical care and specialty referrals. Community Health of South Florida also provides additional services such as dental, obstetric, and gynecological services; mental health substance abuse; and HIV/AIDS testing, treatment, and counseling. This facility tends to service about 3,000 migrant and homeless individuals per year in Miami-Dade County.

Throughout Miami, charitable organizations strive to provide basic essentials for individuals living on the streets, principally clothing. Camillus House consistently holds clothing drives and arranges fundraising events, encouraging large donors to participate in their efforts to improve conditions for the homeless. In a recent Thanksgiving donation drive, a local furniture store, City Furniture, donated 5,500 pairs of new boxer shorts and 3,000 pairs of new socks to the Camillus House program.

Other organizations in the Miami-Dade area that engage in similar programs are the Miami Rescue Mission, St. Vincent De Paul Thrift Shop in Hialeah, Baby City, Douglas Gardens Thrift Shop, and Goodwill Industries of South Florida.

Although some of the homeless in Miami panhandle, they heavily rely on different charitable food providers. The Community Action Agency's Meals on Wheels Program serves up daily balanced meals at selected locations in Miami-Dade, including Northwest Miami, Downtown Miami, Homestead, Naranja, Perrine, Goulds, Opa Locka, and South Miami. If the homeless find it difficult to arrive within the scheduled food delivery time, they can also seek the assistance of the St. Joseph's Church or St. Patrick's Church on Saturday mornings in Miami Beach. Other food suppliers accessible to homeless individuals are Camillus House in downtown Miami, the First United Methodist Church, Temple Beth Shalom in Miami Beach, Salvation Army in several locations throughout Miami, and the Miami Rescue Mission in North Miami.

Homeless individuals who find themselves with no means and little financial support from family and friends can seek free legal advice offered by several community organizations whose purpose is to educate them about their rights and to ensure that they are treated justly. Legal Services of Greater Miami helps the homeless to obtain personal identification documents needed for government benefits and employment through their Homeless Legal Assistance Project. This organization also represents homeless children who may be treated unfairly by school officials as a result of their homelessness. As an example, they represent children in cases which require transportation to the last school attended before becoming homeless, as well as helping to register students in a school without having documentation to provide proof of permanent residence, typically a requirement for a student's enrollment. In addition, they instruct the homeless on ways to obtain food stamps, cash assistance through the Department of Children and Families, and other public benefits.

As one of the major entries for immigrants into the United States, Miami has become home to a large and diverse group of homeless immigrants. These individuals are possibly at more of a disadvantage than other homeless groups due to language barriers and because they are often not informed of their rights. They can seek the free legal counsel of the Florida Immigrant Advocacy Center, which is also charged with facilitating the process in obtaining public benefits.

*   *   *

As we undertook these interviews, we had many preconceptions about being homeless in Miami, as well as many false assumptions. We were probably a little ill-at-ease when first approaching people we did not know, and they probably felt the same way about us. We carried a number of biases and prejudices, most probably related to our privileged positions as researchers. All of us have relatively stable families and have roofs over our heads with sufficient incomes to live comfortably.

As we got to know our interviewees as part of the *StreetWays* project, we realized that they were not that different from most people. To be sure, many had problems with drugs, alcohol, and depression. Some clearly had deeper psychological problems. There were clearly a number of people who were mentally ill in our interview group, but they did not predominate, nor even make up the majority of the people we talked to.

In the end, the subjects we interviewed struck us as people trying to get through life, seeking a future and concerned about making meaning for themselves. Sometimes, they were seeking a better future. Some were trying to find a meaning to their life. Many were deeply religious and carried Bibles with them. We were surprised how many were active readers, since finding reading materials and carrying books around poses a challenge for someone living on the street. At least three or four of the people we interviewed, for example, carried library books. Many made extensive use of the downtown library and talked about the time they spent online researching information and pursuing subjects of interest.

Many of the people we interviewed turned to living on the street as a way of saving money. Roy Taylor, for example, a non-English speaking ex-Nicaraguan revolutionary lives on the street so that he can save money and send it back to family in his village. Michael Farley likes to gamble at the casino in Fort Lauderdale, and uses the money he saves from not paying rent and by getting food at local missions and churches as a means of bankrolling his gambling habit.

*   *   *

The examples provided above, as well as many other insights that we obtained from our interviews, have led us to more fully understand how homelessness is a complex phenomenon that is caused by a wide array of factors which are not always easily understood, especially at first glance. While we do not try to offer solutions to this difficult challenge confronting our nation, we hope that this book offers insight into the lives of these often overlooked and misunderstood members of our society. In addition, we hope that the information provided will help the general Miami community and the nation develop better solutions for addressing the needs of homeless individuals. Finally, we feel that by chronicling the homeless and their stories (both visual and spoken), we can encourage a

meaningful dialogue regarding issues facing the homeless and develop
ways of helping them, while respecting them as human beings, despite
their challenges, limitations, and misfortunes.

Sources

Boydell, K. M., Goering, P., & Morrell-Bellai, T. L. (2000). Narratives of
identity: Re-presentation of self in people who are homeless. *Qualitative Health Research, 10*, 26-38.

Brown, L. (2002). On the outside. *News and Record.*

Buckner, J. C., Bassuk, E. L., & Zima, B. T. (1993). Mental health issues
affecting homeless women: Implications for intervention. *American
Journal of Orthopsychiatry, 63*, 385-399.

Camilus House. (2007). News Detail. Retrieved February 10, 2010, from
http://www.camillushouse.org/news_center/news_detail.php?
ID=134

Centers for Disease Control and Prevention. (2008). *HIV/AIDS in the
United States.* Retrieved February 8, 2010, from http://www.cdc.
gov.

Cohen, M. B., & Wagner, D. (1992). Acting on their own behalf: Affiliation and political mobilization among homeless people. *Journal of
Sociology and Social Welfare, 19*, 21-40.

Drake, R. E., Osher, F. C., & Wallach, M. A. (1991). Homelessness and
dual diagnosis. *American Psychologist, 46*, 1149-1158.

Florida Department of Children and Families. (2009). Homeless conditions in Florida: Annual report for fiscal year 2008-2009. Retrieved
May 5, 2010, from www.dcf.state.fl.us/programs/homelessness/
docs/2009governors_report.pdf

Miami-Dade Homeless Trust (2010). January 26, 2010, Homeless Census Summary of Results. Soon to be available online at http://www. miamidade.gov/homeless/

Miami Coalition for the Homeless, Inc. (2008). Miami-Dade County homeless trust census. Retrieved from http://www.miamihome-less.org/site/files/Homeless_Census_Results_Jan292008.pdf

Miami-Dade County Homeless Trust. (2008). Miami-Dade County community homeless plan: Ten year plan to end homelessness in Miami-Dade county [PowerPoint document]. Retrieved from presentation online at: http://www.miamidade.gov/homeless/.

National Alliance to End Homelessness. (2007). Why is homelessness an important issue? Washington, DC: National Alliance to End Homelessness. Retrieved from http://www.endhomelessness.org/section/data/homelessnessinst

National Alliance to End Homelessness. (2008). The Homelessness Budget. Retrieved February 10, 2010, from http://www.endhomeless-ness.org/files/2115_file_The_Homelessness_Budget.pdf.

National Coalition for the Homeless. (2009). Foreclosure to Homelessness 2009: The forgotten victims of the subprime crisis. Retrieved from http://www.nationalhomeless.org/advocacy/Foreclosureto-Homelessness0609.pdf

National Coalition for the Homeless. (2009). How many people experience homelessness? Retrieved from http://www.nationalhomeless.org/factsheets/index.html

National Coalition for the Homeless. (2009). Who is homeless? Retrieved from http://www.nationalhomeless.org/factsheets/index.html

National Coalition for the Homeless. (2009). Why are people homeless? Retrieved from http://www.nationalhomeless.org/factsheets/index.html

The National Law Center on Homelessness and Poverty. (2004). Homelessness in the United States and the human right to housing. Retrieved from http://www.nlchp.org/index.cfm.

The Council for Affordable and Rural Housing. (n.d.). Homelessness in rural America. Retrieved from www.carh.org

The Urban Institute. (2000). A new look at homelessness in America. Retrieved from www.urban.org.

U.S. Conference of Mayors. (2008). A status report on hunger and homelessness in America's cities. Retrieved from http://usmayors.org/pressreleases/documents/hungerhomelessnessreport_121208.pdf

U.S. Conference of Mayors. (2007). A status report on hunger and homelessness in America's cities. Retrieved from http://www.usmayors.org/uscm/home.asp.

U.S. Conference of Mayors. (2006). A status report on hunger and homelessness in America's cities. Retrieved from http://www.usmayors.org/uscm/home.asp.

U.S. Department of Agriculture, Rural Economic and Community Development. (1996). Rural homelessness: Focusing on the needs of the rural homeless. Washington, DC: Department of Agriculture.

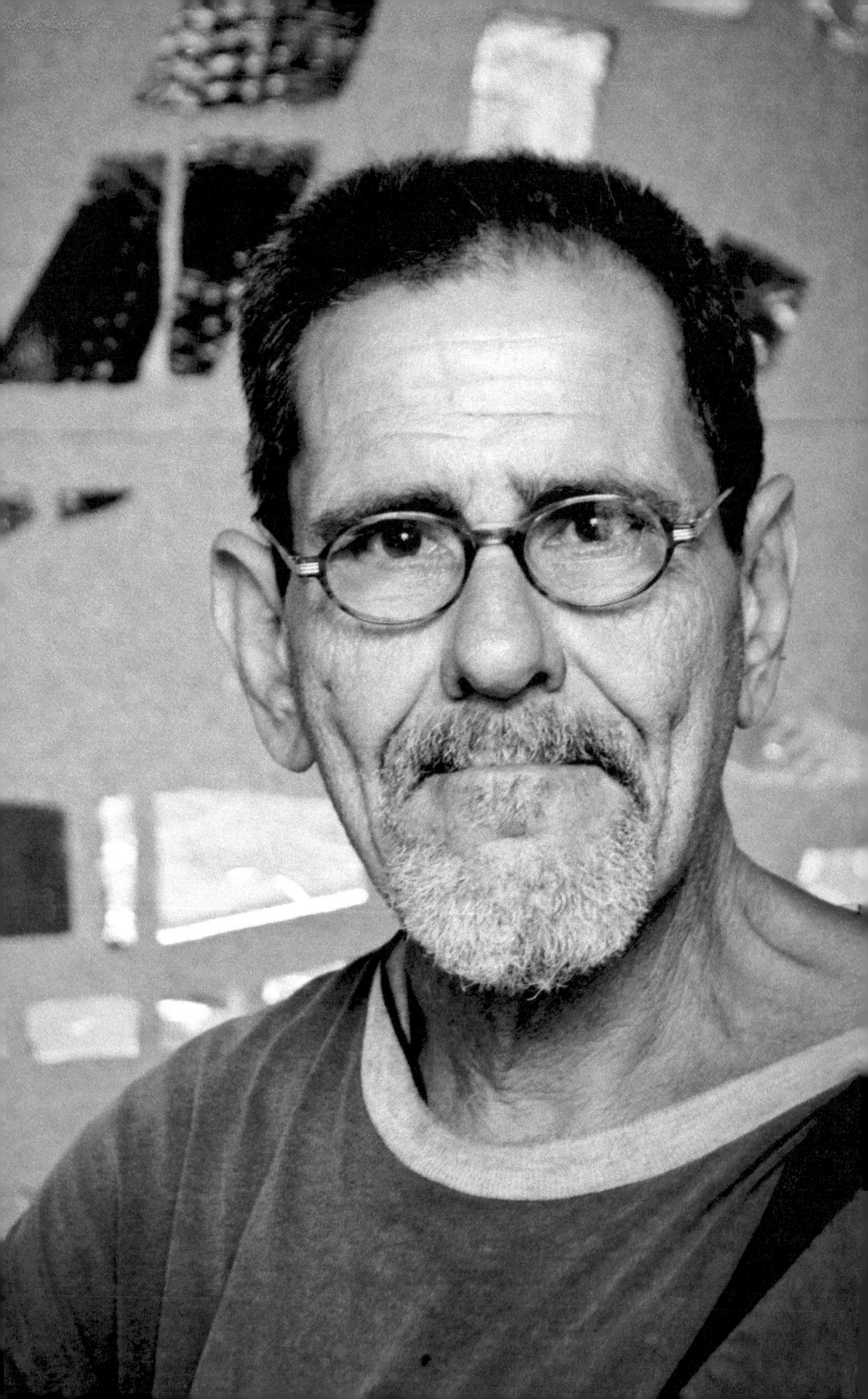

C. A. FRANCO[*]

You don't know how important it is to have a wall and a door and a roof.

* Interview conducted by Eugene F. Provenzo, Jr., Miami, Florida, March 28, 2010

He prefers to be called "C. A." rather than by his first name. He was born in Cuba and came to the United States in October 1961. He is carefully dressed. He has lived in many places, including Washington, D.C. and Arizona. He has a masters degree in Vocational Rehabilitation and a masters in Counseling Psychology. By the late 1980s, he had completed much of the work for a doctoral program but dropped out. In his last year in school he began to go out with a fellow student. After about a year with her, she told him that she was a recovered heroin addict. Shortly after admitting that she had a drug problem, she started using again. She then began to encourage C. A. to use heroin with her.

Little by little she talked me into it. It took her about a good six months. What happened was that on her birthday I said to myself, "Oh you know, let me satisfy her." I knew where I could get some stuff . . . I bought her some for her birthday.

C. A. eventually started doing heroin with his girlfriend on the weekends. After about a year, he went on a week-long vacation with her. This was the critical turning point in his becoming an addict.

I took a vacation. . . . She knew exactly what was happening with me. I did it with her every day. So for a whole week I did it every day. . . . By the time that Sunday came up, I said I wasn't going to do it Monday. . . . I wasn't okay Monday. By 12:00 I was sick as a dog. . . . I went home and guess who was waiting for me at home with a bag of heroin . . . ? She knew exactly what was going to happen.

C. A. called his office and cancelled his appointments for that afternoon. He quickly realized that he was addicted and he got methadone treatment. He felt that the treatment he got over the next five or six years was inadequate—not taking into account research knowledge that was available in the field. C. A. stayed drug-free for eight years and then relapsed in the spring of 2009. He eventually went to detox at the Salvation Army,

but was unhappy with it because of its religious emphasis. C. A. feels that the "War on Drugs" is unrealistic. He believes that policies need to be implemented that emphasize "harm reduction." Drug traffickers should be prosecuted, but not drug addicts, whom he believes are suffering from an illness and who are not criminals.

Then I went to the County, and the County sent me to this program for the homeless. It's based on 12 steps, and these steps are religiously oriented. There are several cases in court that say the government cannot be doing that... You know they were making us pray for breakfast, lunch, and dinner.... "Listen," I said, "I don't mind praying, but that's my own personal shit."

C. A. eventually filed a complaint but got not response. He feels that because of his complaint he was then locked out of several programs, having been marked as a "trouble maker." He has taken to carrying a sophisticated digital recorder in order to collect information on when he thinks service people are not treating him appropriately. Having been drug-free for nearly a year, C.A. now finds himself about to run out of workman's compensation and will not be able to pay for his apartment. He is afraid that he will be back out on the streets again. He can't find work as a counselor since he has several felony convictions for drug possession, vagrancy, and shoplifting.

It becomes a vicious circle. You know I am trying my best to get out.... I go over to therapy... a psychologist. She says, "I see you getting out." I say, "Show me,"... because all of evidence says the opposite.

C. A.'s lease runs out in April. He has turned off the electricity at his apartment, since he does not have any money. He has serious orthopedic problems, which he says make it too hard for him to do manual work, the only type of job he can get. C. A. is apprehensive about going back out on the street. When out on the street, he says it's important to make friends and support one another in order to survive.

You don't know how important it is to have a wall and a door and a roof. Once you are in the air, you are at the mercy of anything that goes by when you are asleep. . . . I wish I didn't have to have gone through this experience. . . . I am a lot less naïve than I used to be. . . . I got beaten, I got shot in the face. . . . talk about safety. Mainly look at me and then look at society and how is that we look at people, and we misunderstand who people are.

In C. A.'s opinion, homeless people are not that different from other people in society. There are good people and bad people, drunk and sober individuals, honest people and thieves. In the end, he feels that they should be judged for who they are, and not simply because they live on the street.

"BOBBIE" OLSON*

I had a disturbing childhood. . . . My father was very abusive in many ways, and my mother just kind of allowed things.

* Interview conducted by Eugene F. Provenzo, Jr. and Edward Ameen, Miami, Florida, February 23, 2010

Roberta Ann Olson (Bobbie) is in her mid-40s. She was born in Leigh-land, Illinois, a small town about 90 miles south of Chicago. Bobbie describes her father as having been abusive to her as a child. As a result, she moved out of when she was 15 and went to live in Parkersburg, West Virginia, where she completed high school. She returned home when she was almost 19. Eventually, she moved to Chicago, Illinois and then Dayton, Ohio. In Dayton she met her husband. About six or seven years ago they came to Miami. He worked as a fundraiser for the Fraternal Order of Police. He died early in 2009.

He was, like, the sole one that worked. We weren't always homeless. When he passed away the money just ran out, and when the money ran out there was no alternative. . . We lived paycheck to paycheck. When he wasn't there, there was no more paycheck. Without any more paycheck, you're not going to be keeping any apartment. They are going to kick you out.

Bobbie had no family to turn to for help. She initially started panhandling in the northern part of Miami in Golden Glades and then migrated down to the Wynwood neighborhood where she had friends. When asked where she stays, Bobbie was reluctant to say, since staying secure is a constant problem for her.

That's one of the things I don't disclose. Because too many things can happen. It's pathetic. They will literally steal the clothes off your back . . . the homeless.

Bobbie explains how she chooses a place to stay.

Lighting. I won't go in abandoned buildings. You don't know who else is going to come in there and then you feel trapped. A lot of it is the police. If they will let you stay somewhere and not harass you.

She dislikes shelters and avoids living in them. She feels they take too much of her money, and dislikes the fact that you have to go in them by 7:00 in the evening and be out by 7:00 in the morning. Police often cause her a problem when she panhandles for money out on the street.

The other day I got ticketed by four different police officers . . . It's an arrest form. And instead of being taken in, you promise that you will go to court.

Appearing in court is difficult. The date for a court appearance is assigned afterwards. Most people on the street get their mail at Camillus House, which is difficult to get to on a daily basis. Bobbie is convinced that home-less people provide an easy "bust" for a lot of police. They represent one of many challenges faced by people living on the street. Other challenges include eating and staying clean.

Just being able to survive every day. To eat. To take a shower. To make sure your things are there if you walk away, if you turn your head. Everything is multiplied by a million out there. Because you can't just put it in your house and lock it up, because there is no house to put it in.

Bobbie describes a typical day as panhandling as long as she can stay out there. People get to know her and bring her things (toiletries, canned food, deodorant), not just simply give her money. Bathrooms are found in a vacant lot, showers are taken for a small amount of money in a local house. Moving is a constant necessity.

If someone finds where you are at, when you walk away to go do something, when you go out to panhandle or to get something to eat or to go to the bathroom, the chances of your things being there are slim to none.

Bobbie has a companion out on the street named Margo (see page 187). They watch out for one another. For a long time they stayed together in a parking lot until they were removed by a local policeman. Bobbie sees all sorts of reasons for people being out on the street—no story is the same. For Bobbie, drugs, specifically heroin, became a problem for her after the death of her husband.

It just deadens everything. But then once you get addicted to it . . . there is no going back.

Bobbie is on methadone, but she finds it hard to get to the clinic (usually by bus) where she has to pay $14 a day on top of the transportation fee. Maintaining a heroin habit costs $50 a day. Most of the money she makes to support her habit is from panhandling. Others "work the street." She sees getting out of living on the street as challenging.

I don't know how to begin really at this point. Once you hit so hard down, it's hard to come up. Just coming up with an apartment. Think of how much that would cost.

Bobbie primarily eats canned food out on the street. When she can, she likes to go to Subway since the food is fresh and considered a bargain. Being better understood by the general public is an important issue for her. She does not think the homeless and their needs are very well understood at all.

Postscript

After her interview, Bobbie suffered a near-death experience. An abscess surrounding a major vessel in her groin burst. According to Margo, her street buddy, "Blood was everywhere; she was white as a sheet and I thought she was dead." Bobbie survived. In her own words, "I am a cat with 30 lives." The stitches sewn up her thigh and across her groin provide a vivid reminder of how close she came to dying.

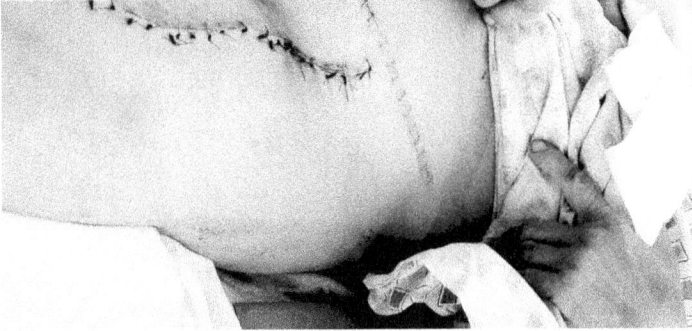

Drug use impairs an addict's veins and makes episodes like this one more likely for Bobbie. When Bobbie showed us her scar a day after her surgery, she was grateful to be alive. A day later, as the post surgery medications wore off, Bobbie's pain levels skyrocketed because of post surgery pain and heroin withdrawal. No heroin fixes were available in the hospital, and hospital pain killers were ineffective because of her addiction.

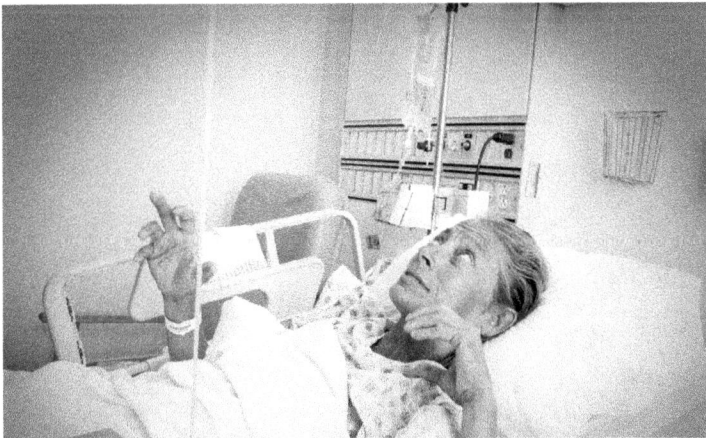

While Bobbie swore through clenching teeth that this was "IT!" and she was going into treatment, as soon as she had clothes and $20, she snuck out of the hospital without discharge papers and prescriptions and went straight to her dealer. This behavior meant that she had to return to the hospital several times to get her prescribed medications.

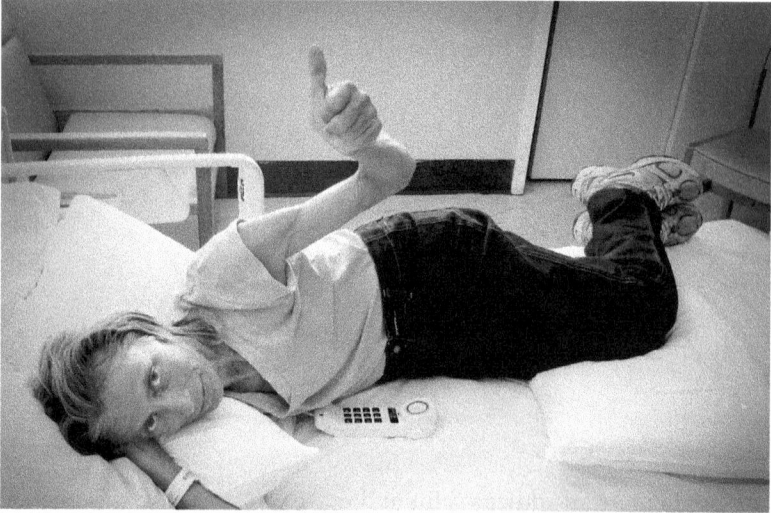

Bobbie now appeared to have recovered. However, her veins would take a long time to heal and continued to be degraded by continued drug abuse. While physically much better, she was still highly vulnerable.

Sadly, On November 17, 2010, Bobbie succumbed to her addictions. A short video about Bobbie and the importance of half-way and three-quarter-way houses can be viewed here: http://vimeo.com/40518680

SERGIO TORRES QUINTANA[*]

Cuando te coge la noche, algunas personas te ro-
ban. Entonces, me dieron un chance aquí. Me di-
jeron, "Mira, Sergio, si tú quieres, guarda tu bara
aquí en la iglesia."

When nightfall arrives, some people rob from
you. Then they gave me a chance here. They said,
"Look, Sergio, if you want, store your fishing rod
here at the church."

---

[*] Interview conducted by Alain Bengochea, Miami, Florida, February 23, 2010

Accustomed to the tropical climate, Sergio Torres Quintana cannot envision a life away from the Miami coastline and its warm breezes. It was the Straits of Florida that provided him the path to freedom that he yearned for while living in Communist Cuba. Sergio was one of 125,000 Cubans who made a critical choice that would define the rest of their lives. The exodus out of the port of Mariel, in Cuba, began on April 21, 1980, and went on for several months thereafter. Living in exile from his native country, Sergio, at age 50, has not yet realized the American dream, which he envisioned as a teenager in Havana, Cuba. Instead, as a homeless person in the United States, he remains segregated by language and culture from the people who had originally opened their doors to him.

Cuando yo vine de Cuba pa' acá, yo tenía 18 años. Ya tengo 50. Entonces, era menor de edad. No me dejaban venir. Entonces yo le dije a mi mamá, "Mira, mami, no me dejan venir para los Estados Unidos." "Si tú no vienes con tu papá o tu mamá aquí, tú no sales de tu país." Entonces yo dije, "Está bien." Busqué a mi mamá. Y vi que mi hermano y mi hermana venían pa' acá, y yo dije yo voy detrás de ti. Ella tenía 17 años. Yo era mayor. Y vine pa' acá atrás de ella. Entonces, vine con otro hermano mío.

When I came from Cuba over here, I was 18 years old. Now I'm 50. Then, I was a minor. They would not let me leave. Then I told my mom, "Look, mom, they don't let me come to the United States." "If you don't come with your dad or your mom here, you don't leave the country." Then I said, "That's fine." I sought out my mom. And I saw that my brother and sister were coming over here, and I said I would follow them. She was 17 years old. I was older. I followed her. Then, I came with my other brother.

Leaving Marianao, a municipality within the city of Havana, Sergio would have never imagined that this would be the last time he stepped foot on the streets of his hometown or that he would never see his mother again. His interaction with her was limited to a single phone conversation.

Mi mamá se quedó en Cuba y entonces ella tuvo que firmar los papeles porque si no, no me dejaban venir. Entonces, me dijeron si tu mamá no viene aquí, no sales de este país. Entonces, llevo a mi mamá pa' allá y ella firmó los papeles. Y vine pa' acá. Ella se quedó en Cuba porque yo tengo tres hermanos más allá. Más pequeños. Hablé una vez por teléfono con ella pero más nunca, todos los papeles como los perdí, las direcciones y todo eso. Espero que esté viva.

My mom stayed in Cuba and then she had to sign the papers because if not, they wouldn't let me leave. Then I took my mom there and she signed the papers. And I came here. She stayed in Cuba because I have three other brothers over there. Younger ones. I spoke once with her over the phone but never again since I lost most of my papers, the addresses and all that. I hope she is alive.

Like the many Cuban immigrants who arrived in the United States, Sergio recognizes that he left behind a great deal. Fearing the volatile situation taking place in a country where sovereignty does not reside with its people, Sergio, along with his mother agreed it would be necessary to escape to the "land of opportunity." Although life has not been easy for Sergio, he believes he is fortunate, especially being able to find employment time and time again.

Cuando llegué aquí, no hablaba inglés pero aprendí. Me fui a Nueva York con una muchacha. Estuve en casa de mi familia. Me dijo vámonos y me fui con ella a Nueva York y trabajaba allá. Trabajaba en una factoría bien grande donde hacían tela de hacer muebles. Después, me fui a otra factoría donde hacía "envelopes" para los Estados Unidos. Entonces me salí. El trabajo no me gustó mucho. No era una cosa . . . Me metí dos años, tres años trabajando allá. Tuve un nene. Se llama igual que yo.

When I arrived here, I didn't speak English but I learned. I went to New York with a lady. I was staying at my family's house. She said, "Let's go," and I went with her to New York, and I worked there. I worked in a really big factory where they made textiles for furniture. Then I went to another factory where I made envelopes for the United States. Then I left. I didn't like the job much. It wasn't a thing . . . I spent two years, three years working there. I had a kid. His name is the same as mine.

Sergio married the woman but experienced marital problems shortly thereafter. They soon decided to separate. He has not heard from her since he left. Wanting to restart his life, he moved to the Florida Keys. Fortunately for Sergio, he has usually managed to find good-natured people willing to provide a helping hand, like the man who spontaneously approached him on a bus.

Me fui a Cayo Hueso, a Key Largo. Entonces, yo venía en la guagua con un amigo mío, un viejito que nos hicimos amigos. Americano. Y entonces me dijo, "Yo te voy a llevar a la casa mía. Yo te puedo llevar a mi casa. Yo te puedo llevar a trabajar en un barco." Yo dije, "Sí?" Y dijo, "Sí. Quieres ir?" Sí. Me enseñó a pescar. Vivía en un apartamento que él tenía que tiene negocios. Y entonces tráileres. Me dijo, "Vas a vivir allí. Ésta es mi hija, ésta es mi señora." Entonces, me cogieron cariño. Trabajé allí. Trabajé dos años con él...en el barco ese. Me levantaban a las dos, a las tres de la mañana. Sacábamos unos pescados grandísimos. Y aprendí y aprendí más que todo el mundo.

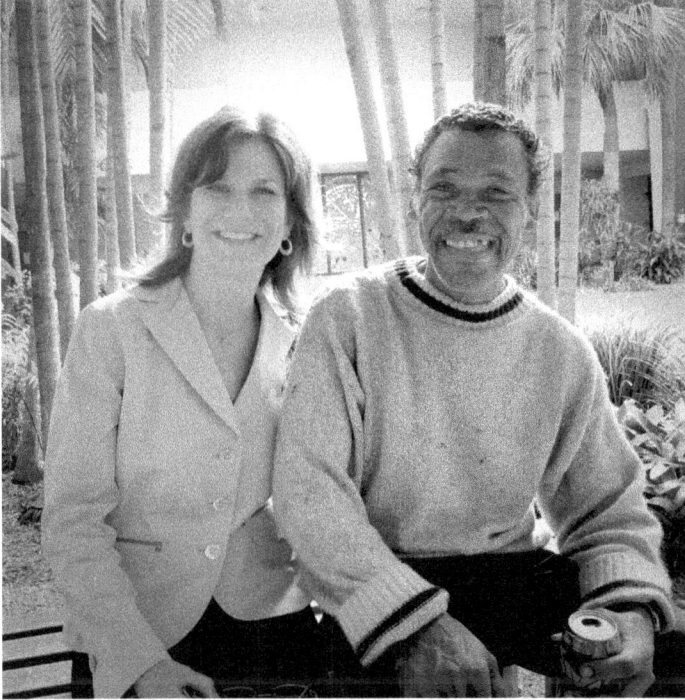

I went to Key West, to Key Largo. Then I was on a bus with a friend of mine. A little old man with whom I became friends. An American. And then he tells me, "I'm going to take you to my house. I can take you to my house. I can take you to work on my boat." I said, "Yeah?" And he said, "Yeah, Want to go?" "Yeah." He taught me to fish. I lived in an apartment in which he had businesses. And then trailers. He said, "You're going to live over there. This is my daughter. This is my wife." Then they warmed up to me. I worked there. I worked two years with him . . . on that boat. They would wake me at two, at three in the morning. We would pull out some huge fish. He began to show me. He showed me how to drive the boat. I learned and learned more than everyone.

He decided to return to Miami after growing tired of the routine lifestyle. The experience as a fisherman has now provided Sergio with a means of survival. Staying near Bicentennial Park in downtown Miami, along the Atlantic coastline, Sergio sets up traps for crabs and lobsters and catches fish as a favorite pastime. Although he never really has had a place to call his own, he ended up living on the streets after a turn of events altered everything. After vacationing with his sister in California, he returned to Miami and discovered through friends that his girlfriend had died from a drug overdose. The only person on whom he could rely was no longer there for him. Not long after, his wallet was stolen along with other important documents that would enable him to secure a job. He began to stay at Camillus House, which he frequented less and less due to the strict rules they impose on the homeless.

Cierran a las 5 p.m. Si tú no estás allí, ya no puedes entrar. A las 6:30 p.m., si tú no estás, ya no puedes entrar. Ellos te levantan a las 7a.m., te lavas la boca y la cara, y pa' fuera. Esos son los mandatorios de ellos. A las 6 p.m., ya no puedes entrar ya.

They close at 5 p.m. If you're not there, you can't enter. At 6:30 p.m,, if you're not there, you can't go in. They wake you at 7 a.m. You brush your teeth and wash your face, and you're out. Those are their rules. At 6 p.m., you can't go in now.

Again, Sergio unexpectedly began receiving help from people who saw something special in him. Much of the assistance he now receives is provided by many of the employees at the First United Methodist Church in downtown Miami. Historically, the church provides health services, clothing, and food for the homeless. They do this and much more for Sergio—they also provide him with regular work.

Me dan comida allí. Sólo las personas que trabajan aquí son personas que pertenecen a la iglesia. Como ahora ellos me han dicho, "Ya tú perteneces aquí. Tú no perteneces a Camillus House." Entonces ellos tienen mis papeles también allí. "Mira, estos papeles hay que guardárselos allí." Dos días a la semana limpiando allá adentro. Y entonces, algunas veces le vacío el carro de los mandados. Como el martes. El martes trabajo un poquito. Me regalan diez pesos. El otro me regala quince. Y así. Algunas veces yo me quedo para que limpie pa' que trabaje un rato aquí. Para que me regalen algo ahí. Me dan dinero, me dan comida, zapatos, ropa.

They give me food there. Only the people that work here are people that belong to the church. Like now they have told me, "You belong here. You no longer belong in Camillus House." Then, they hold my documents there too. "Look, those documents have to be stored here." Two days per week, cleaning there. And then, sometimes I take out the groceries from the car. Like on Tuesday. On Tuesday, I work a little bit. They give me $10. The next [person], they give me $15. And like *that.... At times, I stay to clean, to work a bit here so that they offer me something here. They give me money. They give me food, shoes, clothes...*

Due to the modest efforts made by a group of individuals, Sergio Torres Quintana has managed to get his life back in order. He now holds a driver's license for the first time in his life. He is in the process of obtaining a copy of his Social Security card, which would enable him once again to find work. Just recently, he received professional training as a welder. He hopes to find a position soldering aluminum, once he has the proper documentation, providing him the freedom to live the way he intended upon first arriving to the United States.

BRIAN MICHAUD[*]

Nobody really helps you. Just to eat, just putting food in your stomach. That keeps you surviving, but that's about it. The main thing is that they don't want to bother helping you. They just push you away.

* Interview conducted by Sabrina F. Sembiante, March 30, 2010

Born in Fall River, Massachussetts on June 12, 1967, Brian was the youngest son of four children. A poignant memory from his childhood remains ingrained in his mind to this day. It involves the death of his father with whom he was very close.

My father died when I was 14 years old. That kind of, like, messed me up bad. I was there when he had a stroke, his first stroke. He had cancer, two tumors in the lung, one in the brain.

Throughout his life, Brian had trouble progressing in school because of a learning disability that affected his academic abilities. Schoolwork became increasingly difficult to manage as Brian advanced through high school.

I was in special ed. all my life. I can't read or write. I was born with a birth defect. I made it up to twelfth grade, and I was flunking. I just dropped out.

After leaving high school, Brian found various types of jobs in and around Massachusetts. He worked in a factory that made aluminum light reflectors used on operating tables as well as in an industrial plant that manufactured sealants. He made good wages from these companies and was happy with his work. This would all change, however, when Brian relocated to Florida and moved into an apartment in Homestead with his girlfriend and her mother. He found a job working in the tomato industry near the apartment. After an argument with his girlfriend one day, he moved out, and they went their separate ways.

She moved back to Massachussetts. I told her, "I ain't chasing you all over the world. Stay there. I chased you, I came here, I quit a good job and everything to come," and then she went back. I got rid of her. I spoke to her on the phone after that, but she got another boyfriend, so it was over.

As a result of moving out of the apartment situated close to his work place, Brian lost his job in the tomato industry. He moved up to Miami Beach, was able to secure another job for two years, and rented an apartment nearby. Brian decided to leave this job, however, because his boss was not paying him in a timely fashion. Unable to find permanent work after this, Brian soon became homeless. He has been living on the streets ever since, for longer than he can remember. He has been able to find odd jobs, but none of them has been a reliable source of income.

I used to do dishwashing, but the people never paid me. One day, I worked 22 hours a day, washing dishes for parties, Jewish parties, weddings and stuff. Once the job is done, adiós, no pay. You're not going to get nowhere off them. I even worked cleaning the streets for the Jewish Vocational Center. That was years ago, Miami Beach. That's another homeless shelter or program. I just worked at the Miami Beach Convention Center for one day, last week, putting plants in a U-Haul, taking them away. Work is hard to come by now.

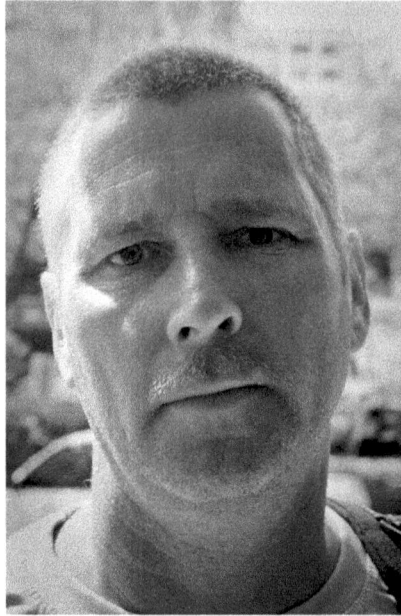

He wishes that services provided to the homeless would include aiding people to find jobs and helping them to put away money into a bank account that could ultimately be used as down payment for a rental apartment. His greatest source of contention is the instability of the jobs he finds and those provided through homeless programs and services.

But when it's after six months, they get ready to make room for another person. You're getting your feet on the ground, and they're throwing you out. They gave me five days and then jacked it down to three days. You can't get no room in three days.

Although Brian knows of the locations of several shelters, he dislikes spending his nights in these places. He complains about the number of people that are accommodated in one room, the smell and the general lack of hygiene of the people living in the quarters, and the petty crime that prevails even in these safer abodes.

Too much people in one room, you've got all 60 that stay inside. I had one girl-friend, somebody broke into her locker. She ended up getting into a fight. I got kicked out with her because I didn't want to see her in the streets by herself. She got torn up. So I just went right along with her.

Brian is apprehensive about the police. He struggles to find a new place to sleep without being harassed and is forced to continually seek out new areas of rest and refuge.

When the cops get to know where my one spot is, they'll harass you—take you to jail for trespassing. You're homeless, they don't like homeless people.

Brian is no longer in touch with his family, who still reside in Massachusetts. Although they could be a potential source of help to him, Brian prefers not to make contact. The last thing he has heard about his family is that his mother, in her eighties, is still alive.

Haven't talked to them in 20 years, or seen any of them. We really don't get along; I won't even bother [to ask them for help]. I don't want to. Leave me alone, I leave you alone. I either make it on my own, or suffer, one of the two.

Brian hopes to eventually secure a long-term job and be able to save money and get a place of his own. His dream is to own a grocery store.

MICHAEL MALICHUK[*]

There's some really young guys out here that shouldn't be out here. They ain't . . . they ain't mental or nothing like that, but as long as they keep staying on the streets, they're gonna get mental.

* Interview conducted by Ryan W. Pontier, Miami, Florida, March 28, 2010

Michael is almost 62. As a young man, he joined the Marines. After leaving the military, he spent time in California, Arizona, Louisiana, and eventually came to Florida. He arrived with friends, with whom he planned to work in the Keys as a shrimper. They chose to settle in Orlando, and gave him the choice of staying in Miami or accompanying them. Because Michael got the opportunity to work as part of the labor pools, he chose to stay and has been here for 35 years. Soon he plans to make some important changes in his life—changes that will get him off the street. His 62nd birthday is in October and he will be eligible to receive Social Security. With this money, he hopes to have the opportunity to rent an inexpensive apartment. He says the VA might even be able to assist him, since he is a veteran. He is excited about the money he will receive from Social Security.

In October I'll be 62. I might not get the biggest check in the world. I worked mostly labor down here 30 years or so. 'Cause I've been a Marine, you know . . . I figure I'll get about $500 a month, you know. And I heard the VA has something that if they see that it's a small amount that you get from Social Security, they add like to make it a minimum of like $600 or 700 dollars. I have to look . . . I have to get the Social Security first then talk to people at the VA.

Michael has been homeless for 10 years, but held jobs for approximately four of those years. Drinking ultimately led to his unemployment and homelessness.

Well, I . . . I have a problem drinking, you know? Alcohol. So that . . . that's probably what that is, you know? I'd be workin' and then get drunk, you know?

Family is not an option for Michael. He hasn't seen any of his relatives since his time in the military. He relies on his friends from the streets.

I know quite a few people, you know. See, a lot of those guys, they used to work. When one didn't work, the other one might, so we'd–afterwards–treat each other. But now, most of us all can only get food stamps. So like now, I get mine like on the 4^{th,} so [with it] . . . I can buy beer and stuff with food stamps. It's illegal. People let you do that. And so I'll find these guys and they find me and then we'll drink. And another day they'll . . . get theirs, then they'll reciprocate.

Even with the help of friends, life on the street poses problems. Michael must constantly find a place to sleep, one where he is safe and warm. Furthermore, he is unable to bathe regularly, especially during bouts of cold weather.

Michael Malichuk   59

*I got a blanket. This church here, on Sundays if they have them . . . I have to get an-
other one. You know, staying clean is hard. Can't uh . . . These places like Camillus House, they . . . they give you a shower, Monday, Wednesday, and Fridays. But,
there's so many people that you get like 30 seconds. I usually go to the beach–the
outdoor showers–but it's been too cold this time of the year. And I . . . I gotta wash
the clothes. I can't get naked or I get arrested.*

When asked why he doesn't use one of the established shelters more often, Michael responded that he doesn't like following the rules that are set
at the shelters. He explains that he feels freer on the streets. Still, Michael
is aware of the situation on the streets, and he worries about others.

*There's some really young guys out here that shouldn't be out here. They ain't . . . they
ain't mental or nothing like that, but as long as they keep staying on the streets,
they're gonna get mental.*

Until he reaches his 62nd birthday and qualifies for his Social Security checks, and possible veteran's benefits, Michael will stay on the streets, living day-to-day, hopefully getting by.

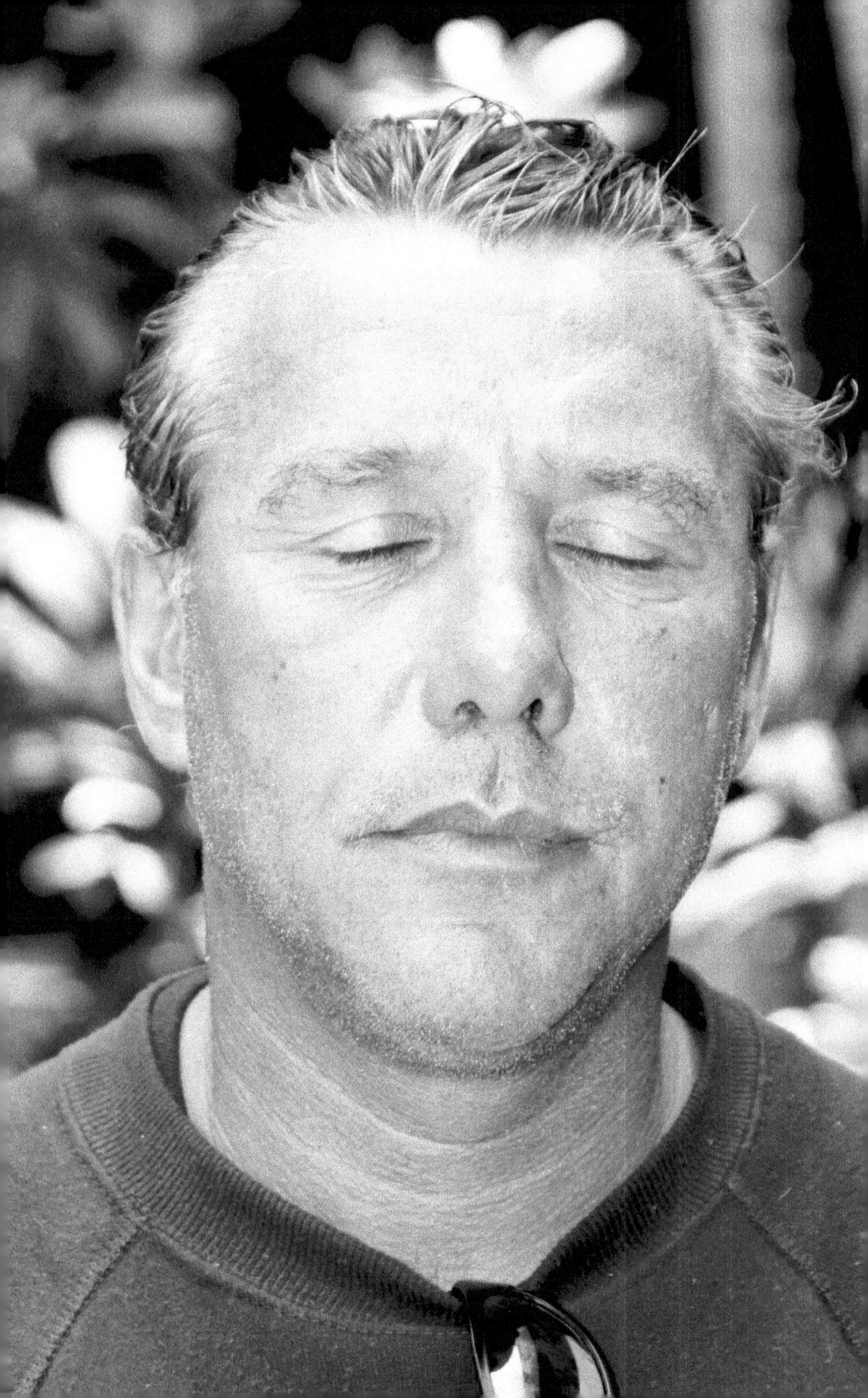

LAWRENCE WIECZOREK[*]

It's terrible, I've only been homeless for three years. If I could take a handful of pills right now and go to sleep, I would do it. I'd rather be dead than live like this.

---

[*] Interview conducted by Sabrina F. Sembiante, Miami, Florida, March 30, 2010.

Lawrence Wieczorek was born and raised in Providence, Rhode Island. Before his father died, when Lawrence was 15, he remembers having a good life, attending camp and school.

I never made it through school because I had to quit in '78 to work, to get a job, to help my mom because I had a single mom. I had to help my mom pay the mortgage and buy food, or we would have been homeless back then. I had to do that to be a dishwasher so that me and my mom would have a house.

Lawrence has been working ever since. Before becoming homeless, he lived in Naples, Florida from 2004 to 2007. He worked in construction, most of which involved manual labor on pools. A health complication in 2007 stopped him in his tracks.

I have high blood pressure and I had a slight stroke, and now I can't do construction work. You need your arms and legs. Now I can only lift my left arm slightly. When I got hurt and injured, Collier County just said "Oh," you know, "go to Miami, they'll help you." They don't want to have nothing to do with you. They paid the first three months of my apartment. Then they didn't want to pay no more. Then I got evicted and I was homeless.

Lawrence has been homeless for the past three years. He is now relying on services provided by Miami-Dade County to survive. He is able to get medicine for his hypertension but is having difficulty receiving his disability check from the government.

I've already filed–they denied me. I have the records to prove that I had a slight stroke. I got all my high blood pressure medicine, I got papers from the doctor, but they said, "You don't qualify." And you know what they put on the paper? They said the only way I can collect Social Security is if I'm blind or dead. What do I need Social Security for if I'm dead?

During his time on the streets, he has experienced much crime and violence. He has lost his teeth, has been hit with baseball bats, and has had severe beatings that have left him with stitches on his head. A broken rib prohibits him from sleeping on his right side. He describes an incident that he witnessed at a soup kitchen where one man, fighting with another, pulled out a box cutter and slit the other man's throat. These experiences have left him scared of others and of sleeping on the streets, especially because his limited mobility hinders him from protecting himself. He usually tries to climb a tree and tie himself in for the night in order to stay off the ground.

While you're sleeping, guys come up to you and start hitting you with sticks and bricks because they think you have money. They just rob you. It's really terrible. Even in the daytime, they'll come and grab your bag. If you got it over your shoul-

der, they'll usually cut the strap and take it. I'm afraid to sleep on the ground. It's terrible, you know. You don't know who's going to walk up on you. Stab you, cut your throat while you're sleeping, take your sneakers off your feet. You know, like, you can't even leave a cup of juice on the table at a soup kitchen—they steal your juice. How low can you be? It's awful man, it's a hell hole out here. You can't even imagine. I have nightmares. I can't even sleep at night.

Although Lawrence visits shelters for the food, clothes, and personal hygiene items that they offer, he prefers not to stay overnight in these locations. He feels that many homeless people don't wash themselves and that the area is rife with disease. Lawrence prides himself on his appearance and does his best to keep clean. He takes showers at Miami Beach and wears his hair neatly combed back. He has found that when he is not well-groomed, people are more judgmental of him.

I ask people, "Can you help me, I'm homeless," and they look at my fingernails and look at me, they say "You're too clean to be homeless." So what am I supposed to do, roll around in the dirt and the mud and don't wash up and stink just to be homeless? I don't think so.

Lawrence dreams of the time when the government will start sending him his disability money. He hopes to go back to Rhode Island, pay for low-income housing and get off the streets. While these are his hopes for the future, Lawrence suffers from severe depression due to his current living situation.

How things are going now, I ain't got no future. I'm better off dead. If I could kill myself right now, I would. But I'm chicken. I don't know how to do it. And I'm not going to spend the rest of my life living on the street. It's already been three years of hell and people look at you, "You're homeless. Oh ,you're a scumbag. You're not working." How can I work? I had a slight stroke because of my high blood pressure. I didn't do nothing wrong. You know, I shouldn't be like this. Thirty-one years of working. So what did I do wrong?

ROY TAYLOR[*]

Día tras día, ando, vengo luchando. Lunes, salgo a luchar más. Y cuando llega viernes sin un centavo, a veces, me pongo a llorar.

Day after day, I go about struggling. Monday, I go out to struggle some more. And when Friday arrives without one cent, at times, I begin to cry.

---

[*] Interview conducted by Alain Bengochea, Miami, Florida, February 23, 2010

With an undying grin and wearing clean, almost starched clothes, one would not perceive Roy Taylor to be part of the homeless community in Miami. He was born in 1960 in Waspan, Nicaragua, a small village that is home to the Native Americans known as Miskitos. According to accounts by his mother, he was named after his grandfather, an American land-owner in Nicaragua who was among the many responsible for exploiting the villagers and their natural resources, primarily mahogany. His mother was left to care for her son with no assistance from anyone including Taylor's father. Growing up in a developing country faced with corruption and marred by civil unrest, Taylor found himself forced into guerrilla warfare, becoming a member of the "Nicaraguan Resistance."

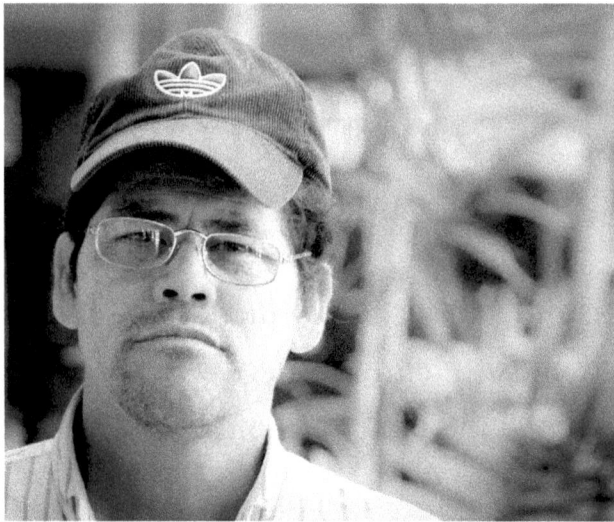

El gobierno Sandinista cuando entró victoria . . . No sé si has oído esa historia de los Miskitos. Los sacaron de su tierra y los trasladaron a las minas y los otros se huyeron de noche a las tierras de Honduras donde hubo guerra. Bueno, a nosotros, bueno, nos tenemos que, cruzamos para Honduras. Y ahí, la Contra . . . Yo tenía como 19 años en el año ochenta. Bueno, me cogieron para la guerra y yo fui entrenado por un americano.

When the Sandinista government became victorious . . . I do not know if you have heard the story of the Miskitos. They removed them from their land and transferred them to the mines, and the others fled in the night to the lands in Honduras where war was taking place. Well, to us, well, we had to, we crossed to Honduras. And there, the Contra . . . I was about 19 years old in 1980. Well, I was recruited for the war and trained by an American.

Realizing that there was no end in sight to the war, Roy was able to escape the battle between President Ortega's armies and the guerrillas. He fled to his hometown where he was persecuted by the Sandinistas for his participation in the guerrilla warfare. His mother, who feared for her son's life, suggested that he leave for the United States.

Me dio una mapa, dice, "Váyase a Managua, después Honduras, después Guatemala, México, a Estados Unidos." Así lo hice. Así llegué hasta Laredo, Texas. Ahí, me recibieron los americanos y me dieron asilo político. Traía la condición, una salvo-conducta, de Tomás Borge Martínez que era el comandante en aquel entonces.

She gave me a map, says, "Go to Managua, then Honduras, then Guatemala, Mexico, to the United States." That is what I did. That is how I arrived in Laredo, Texas. There I was received by the Americans and was given political asylum. I brought with me the condition, a safe-conduct from Tomás Borge Martinez who was the commander during that time.

After becoming a naturalized citizen, Roy Taylor landed multiple jobs working as a day laborer over the next twenty years. He took on jobs in construction, roofing, and picking tomatoes throughout Florida. The temporary positions he held did not provide him with the means to find a permanent home. The belief that there are more job opportunities in the United States, gave him the strength, however, to persist.

Solo resuelvo dos días, tres días pa' comer y mandar algo a mis hijas. Tengo cuatro hijas. Ya no puedo trabajar machete y hacha porque machete y hacha es lo que trabaja los Miskitos. Cuando yo era pequeño, iba con mi abuela, mi abuelita. Y hacha, machete a árbol. Inmensas tumbaban y después sembrar ahí–sembrar maíz, sembrar arroz y esas cosas. Pero ahora, ¿que voy a trabajar en el hacha?

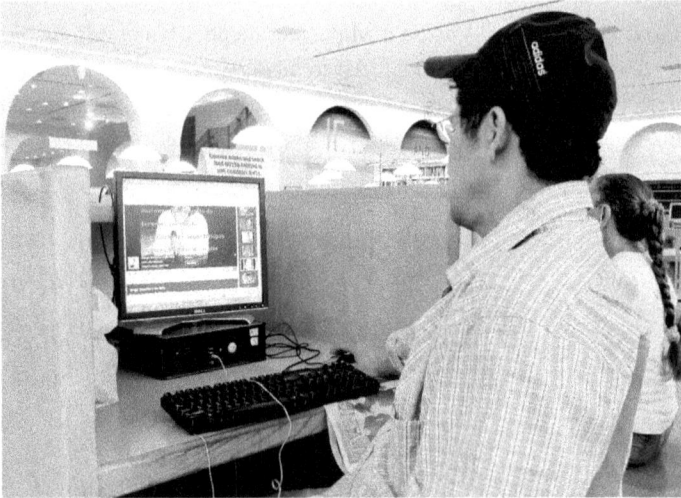

I make ends meet for two days, three days to eat and send money to my daughters. I have four daughters. I can no longer work with a machete and axes because machetes and axes are the work of the Miskitos. When I was young, I would go with my grandmother, my dear grandmother. And axe, machete to the tree. Large ones would fall and then plant there–plant corn, plant rice and those things. But now, how am I going to work with an axe?

Roy Taylor emphasized the disparity between earnable income in Latin American countries and the United States. His cousin, uncles, and sister are well educated and work in the Nicaraguan school system, yet they make exponentially less money than they would if living in the United States.

Ganan un peso al día. Aquí ganan cincuenta al día. Allá ganan tres dólares a la semana. Todos son así. México, tres pesos. Guatemala, tres pesos al día. Todo, aquí. Sólo éste es el paraíso.

They make a dollar a day. Here, they make 50 dollars per day. There, they make three dollars per week. Mexico, three dollars. Guatemala, three dollars a day. Everything, here. Only this is paradise.

According to Roy, many of his dreams are being realized despite the harsh conditions he faces as a homeless individual. Most of the money Taylor makes through day labor work is sent to his family in Nicaragua. He sacrifices any form of comfort to give his mother, wife, and four daughters most of his earned wages.

Cuando voy al Western Union, mandar un dinerito a mi pueblo . . . Ahí, no me importa que me duerma debajo del árbol. Pero cuando no hay nada para ellos, no me importa dormirme en la calle y a veces en un tanque de la basura. Yo ayudé a mi familia comprar sus ganados, sus negocios, y tuve carrito y todas esas cosas. Ahora, me he dado cuenta. Yo creo que sólo me hace un milagro yo saldría de aquí. Un milagro. Yo me quedo para siempre en la calle.

When I go to "Western Union," send some money to my village . . . There, I do not mind sleeping under a tree. But when I have nothing for them, I do not mind sleeping on the street and, other times, in a trash bin. I helped my family buy their cattle, their businesses, and I had a small car and all those things. Now, I realize, I think that only a miracle will get me out of here. A miracle. I will always remain on the street.

For Roy Taylor, saving enough funds to purchase a van for his family would be enough reason to return to his native country. He believes that this goal will not be met easily, however, considering the difficult situation faced by the homeless in securing a steady job and income.

MIKE McCABE[*]

Truthfully, if a person, when I'm out there holding the sign, gives me something, they give it to me. If a person doesn't give, I have to ignore it. If a person gives me something, I have to say, "Well thank you."

[*] Interview conducted by Ryan W. Pontier, Miami, Florida, March 28, 2010

Mike McCabe is 52 years old and has not lived in a home since at least 1977, because of serving time in prison and living on the street. Despite vacillating between prison and homelessness, he has managed to hold a few jobs.

I was put in prison, back in '77. I did 18 years straight. First time. Came out and went back. For about four years. I came out [of prison], and I didn't know what the heck was going on. Back then, I was living up Tampa Bay, Ybor City. I was workin' for a guy that owned a bar. A lot of times, takin' pictures for him. Come Christmastime, I'd be dressed up like Santa Claus. He had me fat and all this kind. He had it hooked up, pillows and all that junk. Up in Ybor City, that's a big part of town, I made money there.

As a child, Mike was overactive. He has come to the conclusion that downers aided him in combating his hyperactivity. Marijuana has also helped him calm down.

I would rather have a joint of marijuana. I've always wanted a depressant . . . ever since I was about [a] 10-year-old kid. And even when I was a 10-year-old kid, 11-year-old kid, they had me taking three valium . . . a day.

Mike McCabe is from the hippy generation and he has strongly clung to what he sees as the core beliefs that emanated from that period.

I grew up hippy, back in the Baby Boomer days and all that shit. But, if [another person] gives me something, I have to say, "Thank you" not "Fuck you." That's how I look at it. Truthfully, if a person, when I'm out there holding the sign, gives me something, they give it to me. If a person doesn't give, I have to ignore it. If a person gives me something, I have to say, "Well, thank you."

When Mike panhandles, he uses a sign that says, "Hungry and my dog needs a beer." He admits to not having a dog and to the fact that the sign has proved useful.

People have just asked me where my dog was. I turn around and tell them I'm the dog. A lot of times I've had people give me twice as much money. 'Cause I was honest.

Mike has firm beliefs on how people should treat each other, and this is the reason for his honesty. He is upset by recent attitudes and actions that he has observed on the street.

It was . . . back then it was "Help one another," not "Hurt one another." "Make love, not war." Now today, it's . . . everybody wants something for nothin'. It's "Gimme, gimme, gimme" for nothin'. Back then it wasn't that way, really. You helped each other. If you help me, I help you.

So why not turn to an established homeless shelter? What keeps Mike away from what the general public assumes to be a safe place and with a meal for those without a home? Mike explained that no matter how inexpensive and small an item might be, there is the potential for it to be stolen in a shelter.

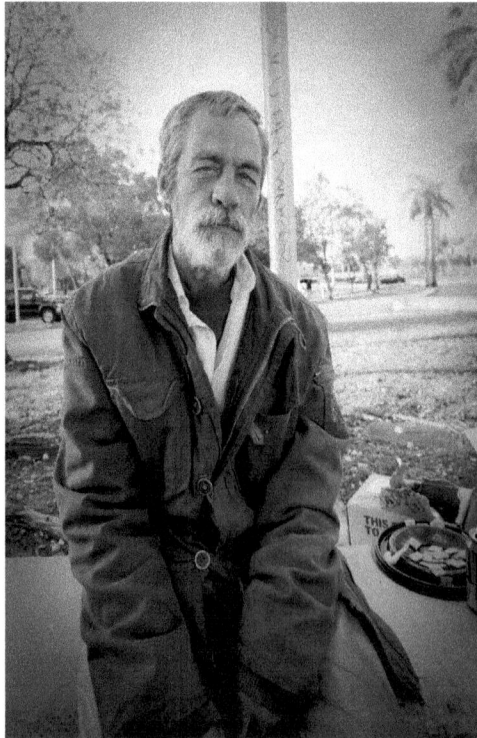

That was where I went first. I stayed there for about five weeks. I've been there two times. The second time I never went in the Camillus House to get myself in. Wherever you go in the Camillus House, people are gonna try to rip you off if it gets them 10 cents. Inside Camillus House or outside. You have to stay out of view.

Mike admits to not having any future plans. All he wants is respect.

I'll do things to help if they help me. It's lack of respect that bothers me.

As more people become aware of the experiences of the homeless, hope-fully the general public will give Mike the respect that he feels he deserves.

MICHAEL FARLEY*

I go up to Haulover Beach and I go to the casinos a lot . . . That's where I spend most of my money. But I make a lot of money. Mostly slots, bingo, I don't do no poker.

* Interview conducted by Eugene F. Provenzo, Jr., Miami, Florida, March 22, 2010.

Michael Farley is 44. He came to Miami in 1987 after having spent some time in California. Since 1999, he has lived on the street for all but two years. He ended up on the streets because he could not afford both rent and food. Michael actually likes living on the street except for the wildlife. Snakes and rats make him nervous. He also hates lightning and finds it hardest to live on the streets in Miami when the rainy season starts, June through November. Michael claims that it is safer for him on the streets if he is by himself. He says this is fine, because he is a bit of a loner. He is also a gambler.

I go up to Haulover Beach and I go to the casinos a lot . . . That's where I spend most of my money. But I make a lot of money. Mostly slots, bingo. I don't do no poker. Now video poker I may do . . . I am laying off it for a while until I get some money—make better use of my money for food.

Michael is a veteran and receives a small disability pension. He also gets a free bus pass. He has hypoglycemia and is concerned about his diet. Most of his food comes from the churches and missions. He thinks the food is really good.

Showers are Monday, Wednesday, Friday, and Saturday at the Mission. . . . . With the humidity factor it makes us stink more. In California the homeless people there don't stink nowhere near as bad as people in Florida because of the humidity factor . . . You won't notice it now, but as soon as the weather gets up . . . the places, the missions, will get really stinky. The missions—really nasty. . . . As soon as the summer comes, I will get my showers on the beach.

Michael has a storage unit where he keeps his things. He spends most of his day at the library. At the library, he reads and spends time on the Internet. He likes to stay close to the downtown shelters where he can get fed. Michael has been arrested for sleeping under bridges, but otherwise he stays out of trouble. He feels that, in general, "the police are all right." Michael wants people to know he is college educated.

I like playing racquet ball . . . I got a B.A. through St. Leo College. I got two years from Catholic University. . . . I'm pretty much a happy person. I like going to the library—having a good time. Mostly I'm a private person. I try to hurt no one. I just take care of myself mostly. I am a little bit too shy for my own good. No relationships last at all.

Michael's inability to function in social settings further depresses him. This happens when he is working with other people. He doesn't have much of a problem when he is out on the street. He observes that getting robbed is common for people out on the street. There are a few things that typically bother him.

Mostly with the rain and the body odor. The work really sucks . . . but I haven't worked in two years.

Michael thinks that the homeless population is handled reasonably well in Miami. He thinks that a lot of people like to live on the street. He would like to see public parks that are designed for homeless people to live in with tents so that they can be protected from the rain. He likes the Homeless Assistance Center's program that has storage space for personal items. Talking to Michael, one senses that he is an intelligent and free-spirited person, who likes living on the street, despite its clear problems and dangers.

BYRON VEST*

I don't want this life. You are in kind of a revolving —you know, a sort of "Catch-22." . . . you know, you get in this squirrel cage and it's hard to get out.

---

* Interview conducted by Eugene F. Provenzo, Jr., Miami Beach, Florida, April 22, 2010

Byron Vest grew up in Colorado. He is 40 and describes his father as an abusive alcoholic. He started drinking and doing drugs as a teenager. He got into trouble because of his drinking and ended up in prison for felony trespassing. He has been out on the street since October of 2009.

Alcohol has just really been a downfall in my life. That's been [my] major downfall. . . . I think I drink more now to cover up the pain of what my life has become. I don't like this life. I don't want this life You are in kind of a revolving—you know, a sort of "Catch-22." . . . You know, you get in this squirrel cage and its hard to get out.

Byron thinks that if he could get off the street he could take care of his drinking problem. He thinks he would need help from a group like Alcoholics Anonymous, but is confident that he could recover. He came to Miami because he was on a cruise with his ex-wife and started drinking when he ran out of pain pills for a severe back problem. His wife had had an alcoholic father and would not put up with his drinking.

So when I drank, she hated it. So I justified why I was doing it. When I got home I kept drinking.... One night I got into an argument with her 19-year-old son about him going to work. The police got called. It didn't turn violent or nothing. She came home. I got kicked out of my home. Next thing you know, I got a restraining order against me. She wants a divorce. I get laid off my job.

Byron came down to Florida hoping that the economy would be better than in Colorado. He has no one to call for help. Byron mostly hangs out with his friend Bill.

We've got the buddy-buddy system. Down here on the street, you don't want to be roaming around alone.

Byron and Bill work at entertaining people on the street.

You make people laugh and they're more apt to give. We do photo ops. You'll see a couple—the wife's taking a picture of her husband—so we'll go up to them and we'll say, "Well, would you both like to be in the picture?" So when you hand them back the camera back you explain to them. "Well, I'm homeless out down here trying to get something to eat. Would you mind helping me out a bit?" And they'll kick you a buck or two.

Byron feels that what would help him the most to get off the street would be to get a haircut, have his beard trimmed, and get some decent clothes that actually fit him, not what he receives from the used clothing piles at the shelter. He mainly wants a chance to get a job and start his life over again.

PEPE MARINO[*]

Drugs for me is like water. You gotta respect water...

[*] Interview conducted by Eugene F. Provenzo, Jr., Miami, Florida, March 28, 2010

Pepe is 53, was born out of wedlock, and raised in Philadelphia by his grandparents. He never met his father and considers himself multicultural due to his Irish and Hispanic heritage. He served in the Marines in Germany and, after getting out of the service, lived in Kansas for 13 years. He was married until about 10 years ago.

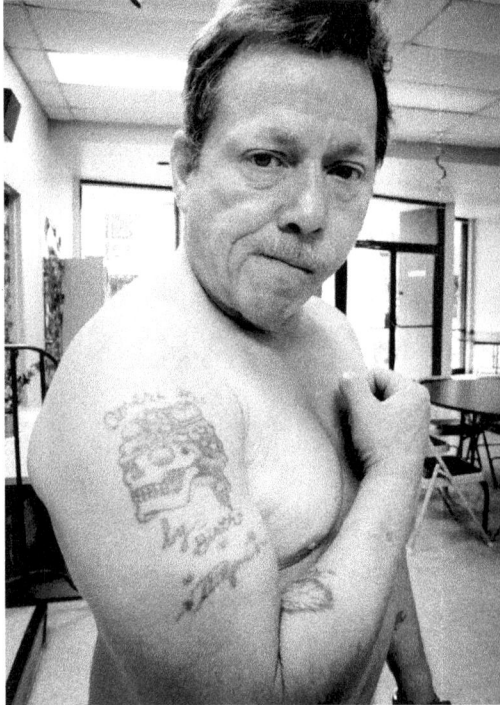

I always wanted to come to Florida.. . . . I'm kind of trying to figure it out as I go along. . . . . I applied for a job at the Rescue Mission. . . . I believe everything is about discipline . . . moderation. Drugs for me is like water. You gotta respect water. . . . My real problem wasn't alcohol. . . . it was drugs.

Pepe wants to keep Miami his home. He has two children—one a boy, who is 18, and a daughter, who is 20. He feels that he has had a tough life. While in the Midwest, Pepe joined Alcoholics Anonymous. Last year he returned to Philadelphia and then came down to Miami a month ago. Pepe moved to the South because he was tired of the snow.

I went through the school of hard knocks . . . I try to stay as low-key as possible. I am an outsider.

Pepe likes to hang out on the River Walk in downtown Miami. He reads novels from the library. He carries everything he owns with him. Pepe thinks outreach groups like Camillus House come off "like a correctional institution or a military institution."

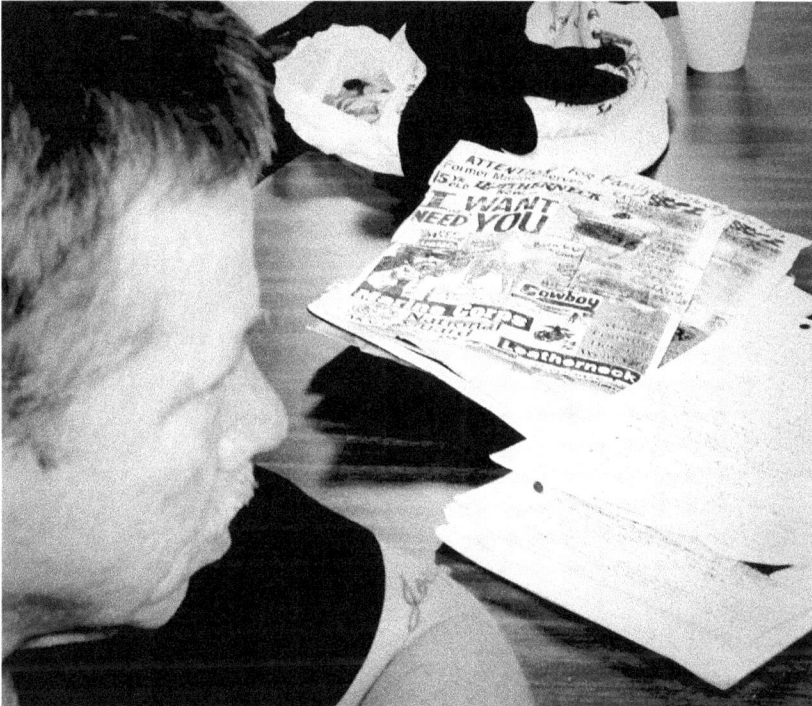

I'm not too comfortable with some of the shelter systems 'cause there are some rough characters. I'm a little guy and I've got an anti-bullying mentality.

Pepe eventually wants to have a career in the arts.

Any kinds of arts—visual arts, performing arts, maybe even literary arts. I am pretty slick . . . I am focused . . . I don't believe in polluting myself with lots of drugs. . . . I don't get into the chemical stuff. It takes too much for me to bounce back. I'm not going to say I am an angel.

He thinks he might have a future working in advertising or working as a cook.

SCOTT PAUMEN[*]

I'm not homeless because I want to be homeless.
I'm homeless because the economics dropped . . .

[*] Interview conducted by Eugene F. Provenzo, Jr., Miami, Florida, March 28, 2010

Scott is 37 and came to Miami from Idaho. He is proud to have lived in or visited 49 of the country's 50 states He has lived in Miami since the end of 2008. Scott came to Miami to be with a girlfriend. He has been homeless for seven months, and ended up on the streets because he lost his job working on the loading dock at the Miami Herald. His life was further complicated when his girlfriend began to develop a drug problem.

We were both working, so we got an apartment together. . . . Right before I lost my job, she lost her job because she busted her knee. She got drunk while at work, and got in a fight with someone . . .

Scott's girlfriend eventually found another job. She spent the money from her first check on crack cocaine, however, and he decided that he needed to move away from her. Wanting more marketable skills, Scott enrolled in an automotive technician training program. He has taken out loans to pay his tuition and now has been in the program for six months. He camps out at the edge of a scout retreat near his training program, which is in the west end of town. On his days off from school, he has been trying to find part-time work. On weekends, he comes down to downtown Miami to get food from the churches and missions. He had a bike for a while that was purchased for him by one of his classmates, but it was eventually stolen. He finds it hard to live out in the open.

Even though he is easily distracted and thinks he probably has Attention Deficit Disorder, Scott is doing well in school.

I am a bit of a neat freak. Living on the street doesn't work at night because I sleep on piles of leaves. That's why I wash every day. I do all right with the laundry, but it doesn't work like a washer. . . . I'm trying to get off the street. . . . Just once in a while, I wake up in the morning and I [think], "I've got this again."

Scott will finish his training in eight or nine months. He gets tired of being hassled by the police, and having his stuff stolen or taken by the police or homeless groups trying to clean up the streets. Scott feels that storage lockers would make a huge difference in his life.

I'm not a drug addict. I'm not homeless because I want to be homeless. I'm homeless because the economics dropped—people started losing jobs . . .

Scott does not have family back in Idaho whom he can call on for help. Occasionally, his mother will send him a debit card, but she has a limited income. He wants people to understand that people like him are homeless not because they want to be homeless or deserve to be homeless, but because of the economic situation, which is beyond their control.

SAMUEL (SAM) PAGANO[*]

They claim a lot of veterans are sick and a lot of homeless are sick. They're not that sick; they're not stupid. They know what's going on.

---

[*] Interview conducted by Kristen Doorn, Miami, Florida, March 28, 2010

Samuel (Sam) Pagano is a World War II veteran. He will be 84 years old this year, although you would never guess it by looking at him. Sam comes from a family of Italian immigrants who came to the United States during the early 1900s looking for a better life. He was born in the Northeast and has lived in cities such as New York, Chicago, and Philadelphia. Currently Sam lives on the streets in various parts of Miami, including Lincoln Road and South Pointe. He has been in South Florida since 1989. At first he was startled when we approached him, but he warmed up as we talked together.

You know what I mean. I saw you coming towards me. I knew something was up. Where I come from, strangers don't come up to strangers. You better know them. Because I'm from a tough neighborhood.

Like his father, who fought during World War I, Sam is proud of how he served his country. He was stationed first as a seaman in Okinawa, and then he was moved over to the Army during World War II. He was one of the younger members of his outfit. He had just completed the 11th grade when he was called up for duty. When he and his unit arrived, they were considered to be the "backup group" because the war was practically over. As a result, he was able to get home sooner. He still feels lucky to have come home alive.

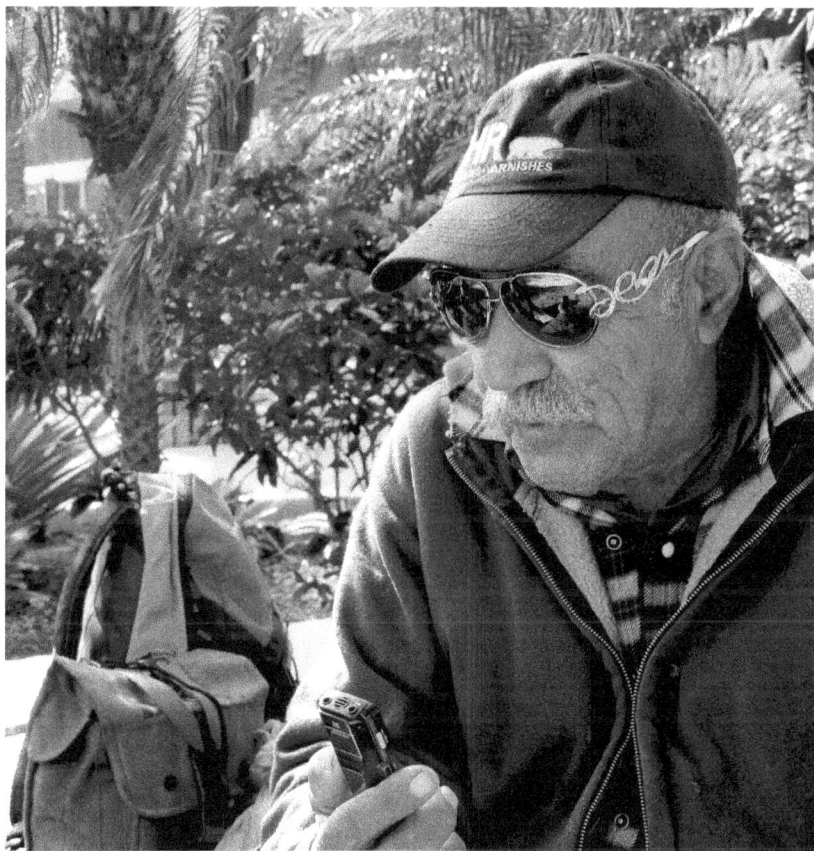

They took the older fellas first, and I was one of the younger ones in my outfit. So I was lucky enough to be born at the right time–1926. World War II was four years, the one I was in. And it was the worst one of all. They lost more men than they did with all the others put together, the way I got it.

In 1946 Sam returned home from the war to the United States. He worked as an apprentice in the family's masonry business. His family, he says, was hardworking but never money-hungry or greedy. Like many who immigrated to the United States, they simply wanted a better life.

They worked for their money. They didn't steal. They lived their life like they did in the old country.

But Samuel became disenchanted with the greed of the powerful and the wealthy. When his grandparents arrived in America, there was respect; now, he says, there is no honor.

So you know, I'm just disappointed in the way the country turned out; because I went over there [during the war] for the very reason that everybody else went over there. To keep it free. Home of the brave. That's all gone.

When asked about being homeless, Sam refers to the number of other war veterans who are also living on the streets. He, like others, receives Social Security payments. This money, he claims, was sufficient for many years and enabled him to pay for a decent place to live. But as time passed, rent has gone up and the cost of living has increased. Now he knows that he can no longer afford to rent an apartment and he does not want to live in a single room. Because of this, he chooses to live on the street, saving hundreds of dollars a month.

I don't feel like paying high rent to the greedy realtors down here who made a racket out of renting a room at the plaza right here that's $550. I see the greed and can't take it.

Samuel thinks the police are too hard on the homeless in Miami. He feels that for many years, the homeless have been antagonized and discriminated against. But he hopes that this might be changing. Many homeless, including homeless veterans, Samuel states, are not sick or crazy. They know what they are doing, and they feel that they have the right, as he does, to live where they want, peacefully and freely. The country also belongs to them, just as it belongs to every person living here. As a veteran who defended the United States during one of the toughest periods of history, he feels that he has earned this right.

SANDERS BROWN, Jr.[*]

Keeping clean. Taking a shower every day. That's the biggest problem.

---

[*] Interview conducted by Ryan W. Pontier, Miami, Florida, March 28, 2010

Sanders Brown, Jr. has been in Miami for approximately 35 years. He was born here, spent some time in South Carolina, and returned. What is interesting is that he does not seem to have a concept of time and does not care to. Sanders claims it does not matter for a person living on the street.

I was born here . . . I'm gonna say, at least 35 years [I've been in Miami]. At least 35 years. But I really don't remember. I don't really have a reason to remember. I think about that now, but it's all documented, of course, I'm sure.

For the past 11 years, Sanders has been in and out of street life. Most recently, he has been homeless for three months. Work, or lack of it, seems to be one of the primary reasons for Sanders' homelessness. He has held a number of jobs in years past, but the results do not vary–he eventually finds himself back on the street.

Well, I worked for the city. I worked for . . . what did I work for? Carnival. What else did I work for? I worked for a company . . . it was a sporting goods place . . . Where else did I work? I don't know if it was Department of Transportation, but

I worked before the Metro Mover was there . . . I had to straighten the plants out. I didn't know anything about no plants, but I straighten the plants out for that. Whatever they told me to do. So I had some decent jobs. I've [had] quite a few. I don't really remember all, but I've had quite a few. But off and on a couple of year[s] I come out for a month or two and usually I'd somehow manage to find my way back, you know?

Life on the streets is not easy. Sanders tries to "stay out of trouble" while finding food or a place to sleep. Establishing and maintaining friendships is also an issue.

So, a typical day would be finding something to eat and trying to stay out of trouble, trying to be humble to people. But I tend to avoid them, because they don't let me have anything. In reference to the friendship is lousy or something or they just don't have nothing nice to say. Reference to sleeping somewhere and the police get in your face. Reference to trespassing or reference to anything or reference to needing money to go somewhere . . . They're trying to label me as a career criminal. I'm not a criminal. I'm just surviving. I've never been a criminal in my life.

According to Sanders, the most difficult aspect of living on the streets is trying to stay clean. Sanders stays away from shelters, becuase of his aversion to crowds. He wishes that there were more public and easily accessible washrooms for the homeless.

Keeping clean. Taking a shower every day. That's the biggest problem. I can't stand it. It's a problem. That's my biggest problem. I wouldn't care if I'm out on the street, as long as I . . . but I can't. . . . I don't like the shelters. I cannot deal

with people. I cannot go to these people, I cannot. So I eventually find a way. I find a way eventually. Sometimes, if it rains hard enough, if it's in the summertime, I tend to take a shower in the rain.

Sanders' hope comes from his mother and his dedication to her. Although she resides close to where Sanders prefers to stay, he maintains a careful distance from her in an effort to shelter her from his difficulties.

The reason I don't leave here [Miami] is because my mom is here. I knew I could pursue other options, but I refuse to leave my mom. A lot of times, sometimes, I've left her and don't contact her for three months. That was kind of hard for her. I was trying to be there every holiday this year. And I think I miss St. Patrick's Day. That's the only one I missed so far. I'm not gonna miss Easter. I told myself I wouldn't miss any holidays this year, and I was pretty good. I didn't miss Christmas, and I didn't miss Thanksgiving, and I didn't miss her birthday. Usually, I've missed those things. Usually, I'm in jail or something at the time. I didn't miss those this year.

Sanders knows that he can receive help from his mother, but he does not want to impose on her. He is devoted to spending time with her during important moments, and he refuses to visit without good news.

She says that no matter what situation I'm in, she's still there . . . I don't stay with her really at all. I tend to not tell her my situation. I tend to . . . I avoid the situation.

Sanders admits that life on the streets is not his preference. Still, he remains positive.

But I try to project positive in reference to the idea of living, and that's important to me in reference to think[ing] about life and others. I really don't think like that [negatively]. A lot of these people that I've studied, they like to be in this situation. I can't stand it. I don't like it at all.

For now, Sanders will focus on finding work so that he can leave the street life behind.

See, my main problem, if I had a job to help me out, I wouldn't be here. My main problem is really financial, reference to anything else . . . And that's what I'm trying to work on.

ELLIS L. KAUCHER[*]

I'm really not homeless. I don't consider myself that way. But I hang with all the homeless people.

[*] Interview conducted by Sabrina F. Sembiante, Miami, Florida, March 30, 2010

Ellis L. Kaucher, who prefers to be called Larry, was born in the West Manayunk neighborhood of Philadelphia and moved to Maple Shade, New Jersey at the age of three. His mother worked for a newspaper company in Camden, and his stepfather worked in Philadelphia. His grandparents owned a large ranch in Cape May. He has many fond memories of spending time there.

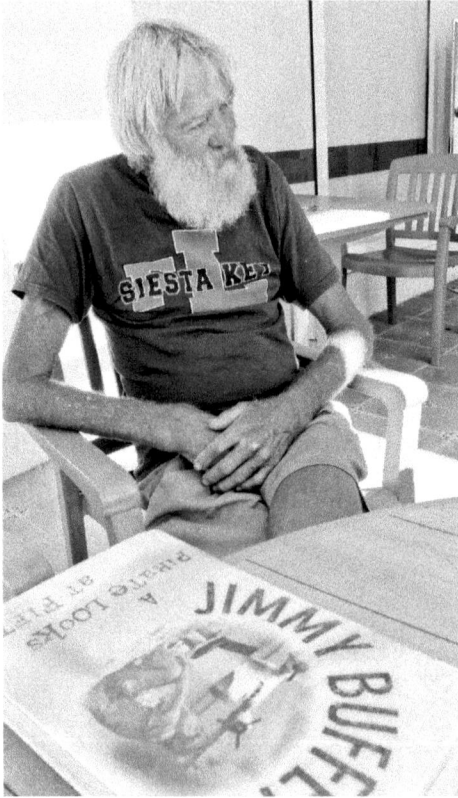

Every weekend we would go to Cape May. Cape May Courthouse was where the ranch or farm was, and I'm talking thousands and thousands of acres—whole fields of corn or tomatoes or cucumbers or beans or whatever we had. I remember taking a tractor and driving forever, you know? . . . Go out there and picking tomatoes. Me and my cousin, we picked two tomatoes and put it in a basket, eat one. Pick two, put in the basket and eat another one. That's how you are when you're a kid. We were about 10 or 12 years old. And [my grandmother] would make big pots of stew up there on her fire-burning kerosene stove.

During his first year in college, Larry was drafted into the Army for the Vietnam war. Preferring the Navy, he enlisted at the office but was not recruited because he was the sole surviving son of the family and was too young at the age of 18 to enlist on his own. He decided to stay in college and worked part-time for an electronic communications company that installed computers and machinery used by NASA.

When I worked for NASA, we built a big container with little electronics that you can shoot missiles off with. It's got a krypton decoder in it. When the government would come in and check it and make sure everything worked, you got about 10 guys standing behind you leaning over your shoulder all in black. When you flip the panel open, it's like everybody's on your back, you can't even move. I'm looking around, and going, "Hey guys, give me a little bit of room here, you know!" because I had to program it. So we built all that crap.

Larry left college after two years with his associates degree because he wanted to do other things in life at that time. He had been interested in boats and the ocean since his youth, and in 1973 bought his own boat to live on. Throughout the years, he has had several types of jobs and been involved in a few illegal and dangerous activities.

I used to do drugs years ago. I used to haul drugs years ago. I'm talking about a 70-foot boat, a commercial boat that's got a lot of room down below to hold fish and whatever, you know? We would go down to Colombia, get off the boat, get up to the shore. We got two 14-foot whalers with engines on them, and I'm standing there and the captain gets out, and he's got his briefcase, with all the money in it, and a first mate. And me and the other mate gets out on the other boat. All of a sudden, here comes about 50 nationals come out and they all got AK-47s pointed at us. And I thought, "Oh, shit. This is a rip off, and we're all dead." I almost peed down my leg. Then here comes these jungle bunnies out of the woods and they got these 80 pound bails of marijuana, and they're just throwing them at us, at the dinghys. I made 25,000 bucks and kicked myself in the butt and said to myself, you know what Larry? I'll never go back for another trip. Twenty-five thousand bucks to get yourself peed down your leg? They could have shot us, taken the money, and hauled ass. I'm calculating in my head what's going to happen here you know, and I said that's not my lifestyle. Ain't even close.

Now, at the age of 64, Larry has been homeless for the past year and a half. He rents a storage space to keep the things that he has accumulated over the years, and also uses the space as a place to sleep. While currently unemployed, he is able to secure independent short-term work doing fiberglass-patching, bottom-cleaning, and painting jobs on boats. He describes his descent into homelessness as a result of indolence.

Pure laziness, I guess. I'm homeless in a way that I don't have my boat cleaned up and ready to go. But I make money, you know? I work. I'm really not homeless. I don't consider myself that way. But I hang with all the homeless people. As soon as I get my boat out of the mechanic shop, I can get on my dinghy and scoot out there and I can start staying on the boat. I guess you wouldn't consider that homeless.

Larry enjoys reading and constantly checks out books from the library. His usual day involves exiting the storage bin at 7 a.m., turning on his radio, and reading a book for the rest of the day. After 7 p.m., he goes back into his storage bin, turns on his night light and continues reading until he goes to sleep. To him, the most challening part of being homeless is the weather when the temperature cools down and the wind picks up. Larry doesn't mind living this way until he gets his boat.

I just got to get my motor out of the shop. I was supposed to do it today, but I don't have enough money, so I'm going to go to tomorrow and see if they'll let me give them another partial payment. It's like a hustling thing. Put money here and put money there and get things done, you know? It's not that I'm hustling—it's the things you gotta think, you gotta work, and what your main goal is and what you want to get. Now I got the boat, I got the motor, I got the dinghy. Now all I need is a generator. That's my next purchase. If I can find a used one, or something like that, I'm good to go.

Larry tries to go visit his mother and his sister at least three or four times a year. They currently live in Tallahassee on a large ranch. Despite his good relationship with them, he refuses to ask for help or to live there in order to escape his current living situation.

They've got a 45-acre ranch-thing out there. I call it a zoo, they call it a ranch, but anyway. They've got geese, turkeys, ducks, chickens, sheep, goats, jackasses. Both my mom and my sister both have money. That's not what I'm looking for. If I can't help myself, it's time for me to quit. [My mom] is a teetotaler—she doesn't drink, doesn't smoke, doesn't cuss. Everybody says, "What the hell are you doing down here, you've got a beautiful ranch up there, all those horses and everything going on." I said, "Yeah right!" You know, I drink my beer every day. I smoke my cigarettes, which she can't handle. How am I going to live like that? Like I'm under a microscope? I can't do that. Plus I love my boats. We're like 18 miles inland on a ranch. There ain't no boats on the dirt out there. So you know, that's what I do.

As Larry is putting away money and working towards getting his boat running, he sees other homeless people who are unable to make good decisions with the money they receive. He tries to help those he can but does not understand why these people do not find work and do not provide the necessities for themselves.

First five people I see in the morning, "Hey, give me a cigarette." "Hey you guys, go get a freakin' job, you know. What's wrong with you? Go panhandle some money. Go bum some money from somebody and buy a pack of cigarettes. The guy gave you $20 the other day. What'd you do? You went right straight to the bar and got stupid." I'll help anybody I can if it's for real. I'll give you money if you really want to go get some food or if you really need something. I'll go buy some food first and give it to them. If I give them three bucks, you know where they're headed? Right to the CVS pharmacy and by a four-pack of beer. I ain't giving you money to go buy drugs. I ain't giving you money to go buy alcohol or cigarettes or something like that.

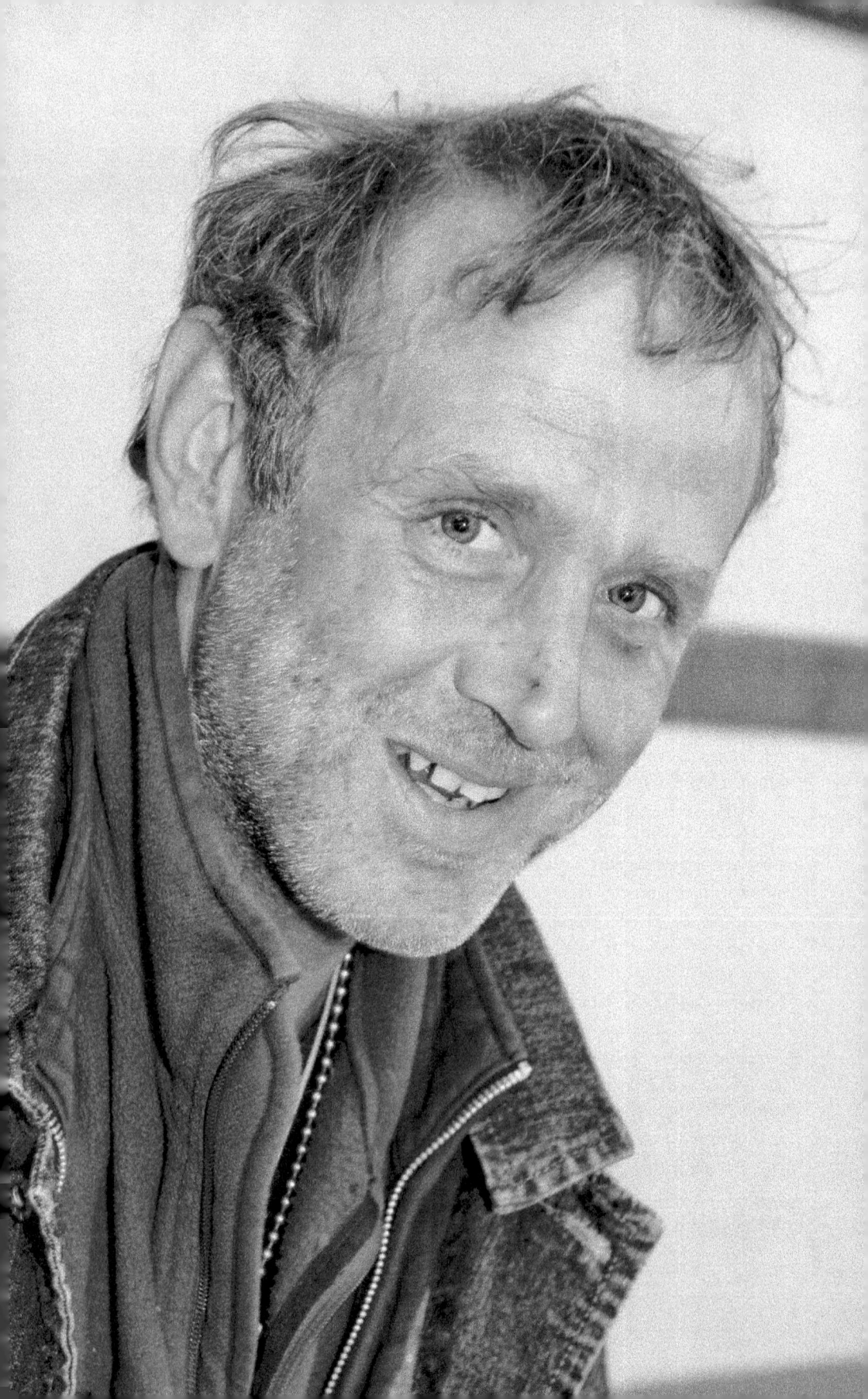

RICHARD STRANG*

I wanted to become a recording star since I was 10 years old, anyway. I was never satisfied with any of the jobs. So I continued to pursue my music dream.

*Interview conducted by Alain Bengochea, Miami, Florida, February 23, 2010

Richard Strang engages anyone who is willing to listen. His unfulfilled desires as a singer and songwriter are the topic of most of his exchanges. Those ambitions are part of a long history dating back to his childhood—a tumultuous time for Strang that has influenced the rest of his life. At age 44, Strang, a California native, resides on the streets of downtown Miami where he has lived for the past three years. Throughout his entire life, he has relied on financial support from friends and family. When that aid was not provided, Strang struggled to make ends meet.

Well, when I was young . . . My mother, my mother . . . I lost my mother in 1970 but not to death. I didn't know. Nobody ever told me. My dad dropped me off at a foster home. I get sent from California to Pittsburgh when I was 4 years old, and I couldn't remember what happened to my mother. But I found out . . . I was living with my mother in California. Then my mother killed someone, but I didn't know it until more recently that she was doing life in prison for murder.

As a parting gift, his father left him with a radio and a harmonica. He began to take up an interest in music, making regular use of the few items that reminded him of his first home.

So I started singing. . . . I had an instrument that I played. I played the clarinet first, then I played the cornet. But I quit them both. Then I had a stereo, and I used to listen to the radio. And I just started singing, singing, singing . . .

And then, it got to when the time that I was 10 years old . . . I was listening . . . That's what I did for my leisure time. By the time I got to high school, I basically almost dropped out of high school. I stayed home to sing everything.

His foster parents, bookstore owners in Michigan, provided a stable environment for Strang's teenage years. The opportunity to remain in a stable home environment ceased, however, when the couple divorced.

I was always seeing the end of the time with the. . . I was adopted eventually. . . . And I knew that the end of the time of living under someone else's roof was rushing towards me all the time, and I was trying to be . . . And headed towards 17, and I was going to be put right out the door because I wasn't these people's natural. . . . Wasn't this lady's . . .

Richard's adoptive grandfather was the sole relative on whom he was able to depend, even past the legal age of 18. As a result, his grandfather's death was a pivotal moment in his life.

I lost an apartment briefly. Mostly started in 1993 when my grandfather died. 1993 started becoming more homelessness because my grandfather used to provide me with enough money to pay a low rent, like $300. Yeah, he was giving me a check to give to my roommate to give to my landlord. When he needed to . . . I've been on assistance off and on. That's when I first became first involved with, like, living, being homeless, but living with people, working for them.

Strang has had difficulty keeping jobs throughout the years due to his dissatisfaction with the pay. Some of the positions he has held include working at Pizza Hut, assisting in window installations, and constructing playgrounds attached to fast food chains around the country.

I never really held a job for more than three months because I never liked the minimum wage. And then when I worked for the people, this guy from the "Playland," he would have me working times when I wasn't doing the "Playland" job because I was staying there. I would work and work and work and work constantly for a little bit of money. So I was never happy with the money situation, which is why I wanted to become a recording star. But I wanted to become a recording star since I was 10 years old, anyway. I was never satisfied with any of the jobs. So I continued to pursue my music dream.

The notion that he can potentially achieve widespread recognition for his musical talent provides him solace in spite of the harsh conditions he faces on the streets. Strang sings the tunes to songs by artists such as Bush and Alanis Morrissette, for whose rise to celebrity he claims to be responsible.

I want people to remember me as a hero . . . You know, risked it all on faith and God. You know, and had everything on the line. A person that helped other people to earn thousands and millions of dollars in the recording business and television and movies and in Hollywood, basically, that otherwise would not have had a job because there is not a big supply of proper music writing hits. It's hard to write a hit song.

Being homeless, Richard Strang taps into the resources available to him. Currently he receives Social Security benefits due to a mental health condition. When those funds are insufficient, he seeks the aid of many individuals he encounters on the streets.

I get a little, like an extra, side check from my head injury and mental condition. I get an extra side check. But, like, sometimes I borrow money or things, whatever. People want to use money . . . that I have, and they get high. You know how expensive crack cocaine is. Well, in just a few hours, you can go through all of your money, and then you're broke. And then I don't leave myself enough for a cup of coffee or anything. Then, sometimes, there are people that will loan me. I've got a *buddy that will loan me 100 if I pay him back 200. Now, I owe $400. When my check comes Thursday, I'll only have $250 left.*

Occasionally unable to purchase his own meals, he relies on organizations such as the First United Methodist Church in downtown Miami to feed himself. Richard Strang prefers the food on the street, often found in less sanitary conditions than that offered by some of the nearby shelters, because of its convenience and the variety available.

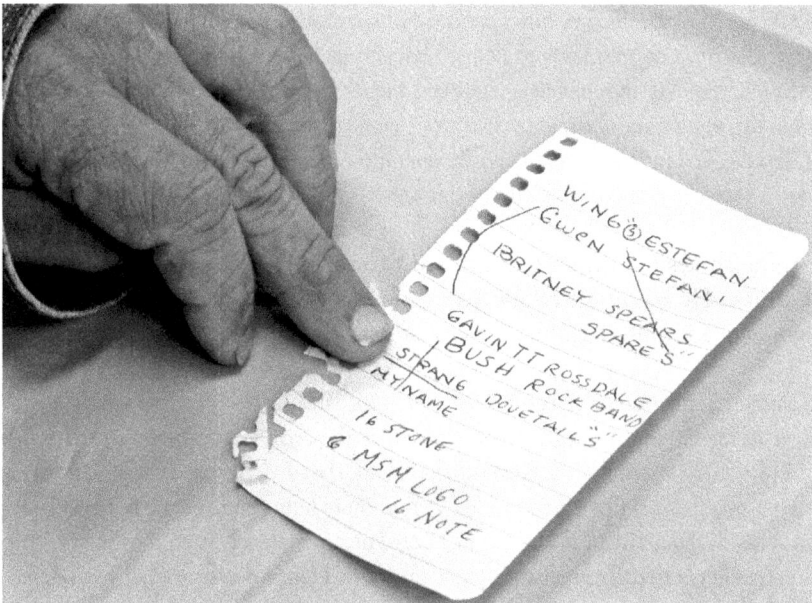

I eat food out of the trashcans and I come to this church on Sundays. And there's food here on Wednesday and Friday morning in a bag. I eat out of the trashcans. I don't like to go and wait for the food, you know, at the shelter places. And some of them . . . the one that's closest by, and the food isn't really what I want. Well, if I keep looking through the cans, I find Chinese, like the trays that people buy where they go for $5.99 and fill up the tray with whatever Oriental, or something like that. I find those. Sometimes, I find a half a cheeseburger. Sometimes, I find a whole one. I find a lot of fries that people throw out. And then, I find a lot of drinks, too.

Although Richard Strang remains segregated in many ways from main-stream society, he demonstrates vast knowledge about current events. In conversation, he is up-to-date on significant events of the past year that would require one to have regular access to electronic media, such as television or the Internet. These topics include the Bernie Madoff ponzi scheme, Katie Couric's move as head anchor to CBS news, the Lehman Brothers collapse, and the Wachovia-Wells Fargo bank merger. One of the current issues in Miami politics discussed by Strang is whether the homeless will be forced out of the downtown area in an effort to move them away from the luxury high-rise apartments being constructed.

They're trying to move them out of the downtown area. You're asking about what I see for Miami's future, but I've had business ideas down here, but things happen. Because the residents of Miami have to be here to support the businesses of Miami. And so the homeless . . . And the businesses . . . So if you're not being able to support the businesses with any money, you shouldn't be sleeping in the sidewalks, urinating, using the bathroom on the sidewalks. But they're all sleeping down there, just two blocks away from there.

Strang shows resentment and distrust toward many in the homeless community. He has endured a broken cheekbone as well as lesions from violent acts commited against him by other individuals on the street.

Sometimes, it can involve being drunk and just wanting to fight. Just taking advantage of me circumstantially because, because they can get away with it. Because they know how much . . . Because they sense that I don't trust them. They pick up on my . . . It's a psychic kind of . . . You know how people don't put everything into words. Sometimes, things are just acted out in violence when they're not really . . . There isn't really any cause other than . . . Here we are together but we may be really, you know . . . It's, it's like a . . . This is like a lifelong kind of a tragedy.

Richard Strang remains optimistic about his future. He hopes to save the money he would ordinarily squander in the first few weeks and, instead, economize so it lasts an entire month. He plans to do this until he gains recognition for his musical talents as a singer and songwriter.

JEFFREY ALLEN WILLIAMS*

It's [a] full-time job being homeless. It's like war. It is terrifying.

* Interview conducted by Eugene F. Provenzo, Jr., Miami, Florida, March 30, 2010

Jeffrey Allen Williams is 42 years of age. He lives on the street with his fiancee, whom he has been with for the past three years. He is originally from Dallas, Texas and has lived in various parts of the country as far away tas Seattle, Washington, where he was before he came to Miami. He came to Miami two and a half months ago to look for his older brother, who has psycholgical problems and whose last known location was Miami. Jeffrey has been denied access to homeless shelters because he is a registered sex offender. He feels strongly that this designation is not only unfair but has literally ruined his life.

I am a registered sex offender, and the government has forgotten about us. This happened in 1988. . . . Hey, government, you guys forgot about me! I had a girlfriend in 1988 and retroactively you have ruined my life by the retroactive laws. I can't get a job. I can't even get into a homeless shelter. A homeless shelter won't even take me. So now, what am I supposed to do, Mr. President, or whoever made those laws? I know that people who do bad things, like pamper sniffers and crazy creeps like that, deserve to be punished. This was my girlfrriend in 1988.

Jeffrey's girlfriend was 15 and he was 19. His involvement with her led to his conviction as a level-one sex offender, a designation he believes that he is stuck with. While he admits that he was wrong in what he did, he felt that it is something he should not have to carry with him for the rest of his life.

I don't think I can even get a job at McDonald's anymore. I am a level-zero in Arizona. . . . I can't afford a lawyer. The retroactive law shouldn't even affect me. I signed a plea agreement. I said, "I'm guilty." Later they made Megan's Law. And that means I had to register.

Jeffrey carries a guitar with him on the street. He talks about working as a professional musician. At the end of our interview, he played a song about one of his girlfriends. He is clearly talented, perhaps even gifted.

I am a professional musician. I have been playing Hard Rock Cafes. I tried to quit drinking and doing drugs—get in the business. Nobody will hire me because of the record.

Jeffrey attributes his drinking and his use of drugs to an abusive father.

My dad gave me alcohol when I was young, and he gave me acid when I was 8. . . . Thought it was funny. He was a knucklehead. . . . Playing in a rock-and-roll band I have done drugs . . . coke, crank, heroin . . . MDMA . . . I am trying to get a hand up, not a handout.

Jeffrey feels that the laws need to be changed. He cannot afford a lawyer and very much wants to get off the street. It is his feeling that the law has been harsher dealing with him than with many murderers.He is living in a park in Little Haiti and is constantly in fear of what might happen to him on the street.

I heard gunshots last night sleeping in the park. We heard an AK-47 go off. A child and her mother were killed. And I heard the shots that killed them. . . . You've got to be always looking behind your back. . . . . It's [a] full-time job being homeless. It's like war. It is terrifying.

He says that he needs transportation to get to the homeless shelters downtown, that he needs a place to shower and leave his things in a safe place.

I pray to God that I can lift this ton of bricks off of me that I have been living with since I was 19 years old. Me and my fiancee having a small apartment. It doesn't need to be that large, just somewhere to hang my hat.

Jeffrey's needs seem simple and straightforward, yet extremely difficult to achieve— basically a home and safe place to live.

WAYNE EDWARDS, SR. [*]

Nothing is better than having your own door keys.

[*] Interview conducted by Eugene F. Provenzo, Jr. Miami, Florida, April 10, 2010

Wayne Edwards, Sr. is 52 years of age. He is originally from Pittsburgh, Pennsylvania and has been living in Miami for a year, having come down to avoid the snow. He attributes his homelessness to his recent divorce. He expects to get off of the street as soon as he can get a job in construction. Wayne has had problems with alcohol and drugs. For a while he worked as a street dealer.

I don't have anything against it. That's what makes the world go around, money and drugs. . . . First started out with marijuana, of course, then powder and then started doing crack.

Wayne has been arrested twice for dealing marijuana. He is scared of getting arrested a third time and ending up in jail permanently. Trying to steer clear of any trouble, he spends a lot of his time at the library.

Nothing is better than having your own door keys. . . . . I get tired of getting told when to get a shower and when to eat.

Wayne describes living on the streets in Miami as involving "a lot of killing." According to Wayne, some homeless people, particularly those with mental problems, will prey on others who are homeless, often stealing and fighting.

He thinks that a lot more opportunities ought to be provided to kids before they end up on the street.

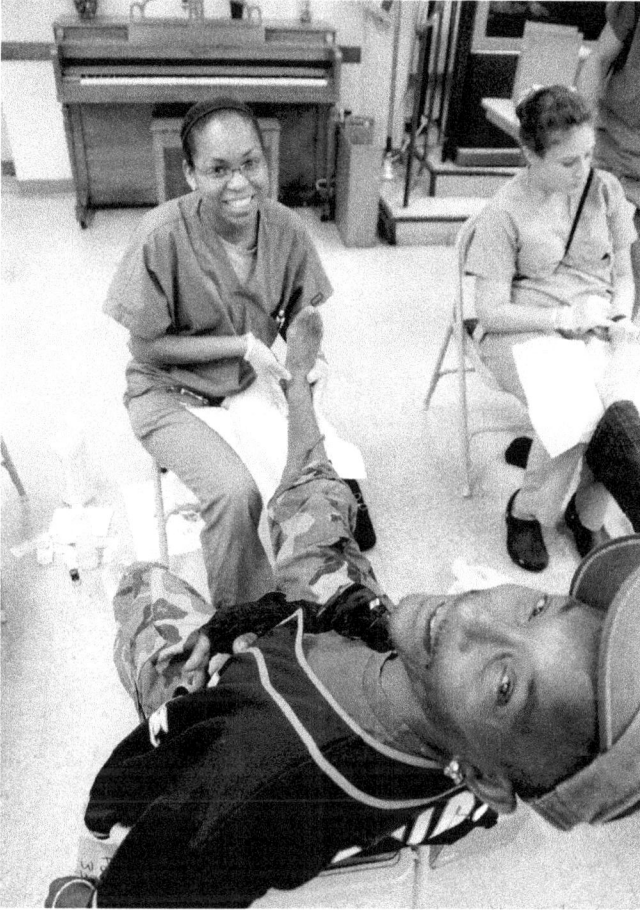

I think they should, like, when I was in Harrisburg . . . They should give you, like, when you are 16, a summer job.

Wayne hopes to get a job at a local pizza shop. Eventually, he would like to earn enough so that he can own a Hummer or a Jaguar sedan.

ELLIS "SONNY" HAYNES[*]

I know I'm desperate. It's like the piece of a puzzle; it has to happen.

* Interview conducted by Kristen Doorn, Miami, Florida, March 28, 2010

His real name is Ellis Haynes, but he likes to go by Sonny. He is clean-shaven and neatly dressed and is a quiet and reserved individual. However, when he speaks about his true passion, music, his initial timidity disappears. It is immediately evident that it is this passion that brought him to the Miami area less than two years ago. Previously he lived in Louisiana, where he worked as a carpenter building houses. Even though he liked the stability of a steady paycheck, he knew that he had to follow his dream.

Someone was telling me that I can't do that and try to promote my music at the same time. So I sacrificed my job in Louisiana and bought a ticket here.

Sonny loves to talk about his music. He became interested in it at an early age, when he started out as a percussionist.

It's just like that movie Phenomenon *with John Travolta, where the ray of light blessed him. Somehow or another I was blessed. And it was just like the flick of a switch.*

From there, his love of the art form has grown. He considers himself a creator, and he is waiting for that "big break." He has several albums ready for production. He is just waiting for the opportunity to work with more established musicians.

I'm a different type of writer. I come up with the themes in the songs and some of the videos, the covers. I haven't really sat down and wrote some of the lyrics yet. I want to sit with the musician so they put their style with my style. . . . Everybody's happy.

Even though his dream is to find work in the music industry, he realizes it is an ambitious goal. Meanwhile, he is looking for other work so that he has the means to provide for himself while he continues to search for an opportunity in the entertainment field. He arrived in Miami during one of the roughest economic downturns in our nation's history, and he has not been able to find steady employment since. However, when asked if he ever regrets leaving his home in Louisiana to move to South Florida in order to pursue his dreams, he answers without hesitation.

No, never do . . . I know I'm desperate. It's like the piece of a puzzle; it has to happen.

Sonny, like many of the homeless individuals in Miami, prefers to live on the street rather than stay in shelters. Even though he has been robbed a few times, he still says he prefers to live outside. He has resorted to carrying his belongings with him wherever he goes, as he fears they might get taken.

I tried the shelters, but it's the intellect inside . . . Some of the clients there, they have no common sense or respect or nothing for anybody or their selves. It's kind of hard to be around that all the time, I just had to get away.

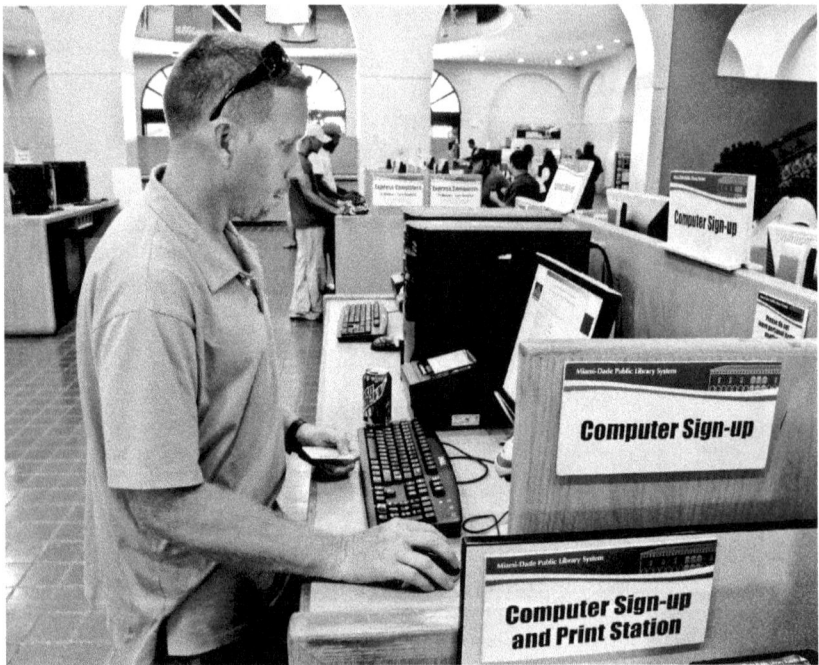

He uses the downtown library to check his e-mail, read, and do research. He goes to Camillus House and other missions to take a shower and get a good meal to sustain him as he looks for employment. He would be willing to use some of the shelters, he stated, if they had different guidelines for the individuals who stay there. He believes that the shelters and missions should try to offer homeless individuals a grace period to try to secure a job and to better their financial situations.

But what it is, all the rescue missions are full right now. That's why there's so many people on the street right now. So, if we had another mission, I think that would really clean [up] the streets.

Sonny's ultimate goal is to set up a production company, Camelot Studios, first in Miami and later in Louisiana. He has already designed the logo, which is the arm of a king's knight with his shining silver sword and has the word "Camelot" written underneath. In addition to his musical creations, he has thought of ideas and themes for numerous movie scripts based on shows like CSI Miami and Las Vegas, with characters chosen and actors assigned. But he claims that it is hard to get in contact with production managers and studios, as they are not accepting new material because of the economic downturn, resulting in a slowdown in the entertainment industry.

But most of the time they won't even send it back if they're not even interested. I have to try to call them and maybe talk to an agent or something, a manager or something.

In the meantime, Sonny continues to wait, patient and hopeful, never losing sight of the dream which brought him to South Florida.

RANDY CHAPMAN*

And I'm not a bad person, I'm a kind loving person. But I get walked on like a doormat. I've got no backbone—that's the problem.

---

* Interview conducted by Kristen Doorn, Miami, Florida, March 28, 2010

Randy Chapman was born in Bedford, Indiana and moved to Kentucky as a teenager. A reflective and observant individual, he is open to chatting about his life, although one quickly realizes that his is a difficult story to tell. He moved to Miami in September of 1973 after running away from home. Randy is an alcoholic. He started drinking when he first moved to Miami in his teens, and his life has been plagued by the disease of alcoholism ever since. He understands quite well the difficulty of fighting the disease and how hard it can be to live with it daily.

When I came down here, I was 17. That's when I started the drinking. Although it wasn't as bad as it is now, it got worse. It's a progressive disease for some. When you have blackouts after three or four beers, you know something's not quite right. Then, that's the alcoholic in you that keeps going and going and going.

He attributes the beginning of his drinking habit, as well as his homelessness, to the difficult home life he experienced as a child and teenager. Randy was beaten by his father, who was also an alcoholic.

Same thing with the drinking and beating your wife, your children, whichever. And I was an abused child. And I witnessed my mother being beaten countless numbers of times. Every weekend over a period from the time I was about 4 years old until he took his life when I was 11, I witnessed that every weekend. You multiply that by 52 weeks in a year and see what you come up with. Every weekend, from Friday night till Sunday, he drank and drank and smacked her around.

His mother finally divorced his father when Randy was young. Later his father committed suicide. However, the absence of Randy's father in his life offered him no refuge from the abuse, as his mother continued the beatings. When he was later placed in a foster home, he was subjected to more physical abuse by his foster mother.

It's not that you dwell on it. It's just there. . . . I think what I went through, it destroyed my emotional makeup is what I think.

Randy lives alone because he feels that it is difficult to both find and keep friends when you are homeless. He has been robbed and beaten numerous times by other homeless individuals and criminals who roam the streets, and he feels that he cannot trust anyone except himself.

You have no friends. I have no friends. Period.

He has earned money for food, as well as money to support his drinking habit, by participating in clinical trials for different types of medicine. He has made as much as $60 to a $100 a day, participating in research for organizations like Seaview, the University of Miami, and Hanley Hazelton in West Palm Beach. But because of severe damage to his throat, he is no longer able to participate, as the medication actually becomes lodged in his throat when he tries to swallow. He has had surgery twice to correct the problem, but he still has difficulty swallowing and breathing. The only recourse for taking any type of medication is dissolving it in water.

In fact the doctor says I shouldn't drink at all. Not only because I get bombed out of my mind, but because it gets my throat to actually bleeding. That's how much damage I have.

Randy suffers from additional ailments, as well. He has a hernia and en-larged prostate, which he believes is probably cancerous. He also suffers from serious depression and anxiety, and he attempted suicide when he was younger. Although he says that he is entitled to disability payments because of his health conditions and injuries, he has never received them. Because of the serious physical and emotional distress that he has suf-fered, he has to take pills on a regular basis to help him sleep at night.

I know at least 10 different people that get a check, and neither one of those things is wrong with them. Yet, they get it. And I got all that. I've talked to several people and they say I should be getting it, but I don't.

Randy believes that the hardest thing about being homeless is his experi-ences with being robbed and beaten; he realizes it's a dangerous life, living on the streets. In October 2006, he was the victim of a serious mugging and beating. He spent three weeks in Jackson Memorial Hospital while his body healed.

They had to do surgery on my face. They fractured my leg, and to this day, I still have pain. It never healed right.

Like many other homeless in Miami, he would rather live outside on the streets than in one of the homeless shelters or missions in the area.

The only difference between all of them [the homeless shelters] is that they cut out the Bible and went straight for the money. That's the only difference. I know from being in some. It's about, like, . . .helping the homeless is big business. And it's not about helping, it's exploiting the situation. All of them, it's nothing but a den of thieves.

In accordance with the opinions of many other homeless in Miami, he feels that the Miami police antagonize the homeless, forcing them to move their belongings and sometimes destroying their personal property.

The [shelter] or jail, now that's really a choice, is it? Naturally, you'll take the [shelter] rather than go to jail, right? That's Miami's finest for you.

Randy just celebrated his 54th birthday at the beginning of March. He hopes for a better year ahead.

PATRICK REMPKOWSKI[*]

It's not because I can't keep a job. It's because they won't give me a job.

[*] Interview conducted by Alain Bengochea, Miami, Florida, March 28, 2010

Wary of whom he speaks to, he finds it difficult to recount what has led him to this point in his life. At age 53, Patrick Rempkowski refuses to seek new friends and associate with people he does not know. Instead, he relies on the few individuals who guarantee him work, enabling him to steer clear of possible trouble on the street. Originally from Elizabeth, New Jersey, Patrick tends to change location in an attempt to avoid potential altercations with police. Some of the states in which he has lived include California, the Carolinas, Florida, Georgia, Texas, and Virginia.

Every now and then, I like to hike across the United States. I like to go to California. I've been all over the United States . . . to get out of here for a while. It gets old for a while and the harassment you get. . . . Instead of it saying "Professional Law Enforcement" on the back corner panel of their police cars, it should say "Professional Law Harassment." They give me so much harassment, and all I have to be doing is walking along the street or riding my bicycle, and they'll come and mess with me.

Patrick's resentment toward law enforcement officials may be attributed to the run-ins he has had with police while living on the streets.

He believes police officers show no sympathy for the homeless, who are just trying to survive. Having been convicted three times for crimes he now regrets, Patrick feels he had no other option.

It's us and them. I was in dire need and did stupid things, which I'm not proud of or nothing to tell your grandchildren about. It was stupidity. It was a needful thing because you need to eat, you need certain things, you know. Just to survive out there. Even to survive out here, you can't just be out here—you've got to hustle.

Patrick admits he is not happy about sharing the experiences that made him a three-time convicted felon and wishes he had never resorted to any illegal actions in his past, including breaking and entering. Fortunately, Patrick has built friendships over the years with a few people who offer him work time and again, which in turn, has helped to keep him out of trouble.

I make the rounds of some of the people I help out. They help me out. I walk Mr. Ross' dog for him and he'll give me five bucks. He's down here down the road. I go to the Food Spot on Bird Road. See who's working there. The owner or one of the counter people that work in there . . . They usually give me odd jobs to do like stock shelves . . . take the garbage out. Things like that.

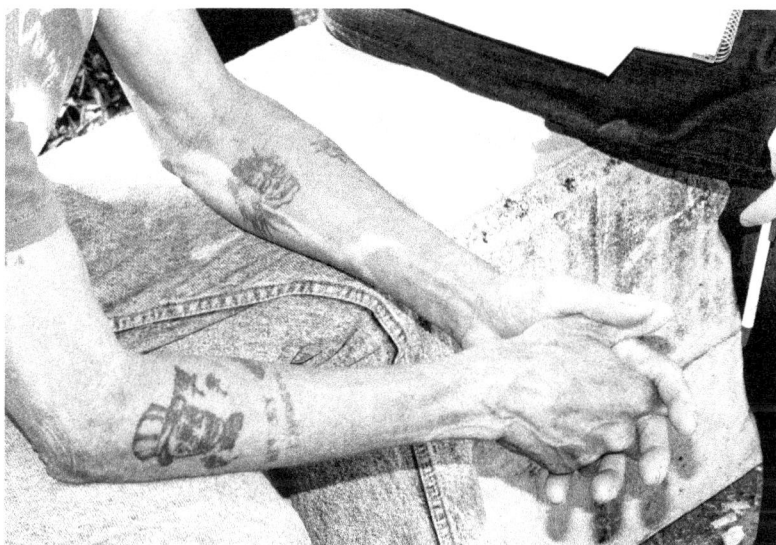

According to Patrick, few opportunities are given to people with a criminal record.

That's another deterrent for them giving me a job. When you're filling out applications, it asks you on there, "Have you ever been arrested and for what?" So you know, who do you think they're going to give the job to? You? They're not going to give the job to me. I've put out so many applications, I can do them blindfolded.

Since a very young age, Patrick Rempkowski has faced hardship without the earnest guidance of anyone who could have possibly thwarted his unlawful activity.

I've been living on the streets since I was 11 years old. My father died, and he was only 39. He was a cross-country trucker. My mother just told me to haul ass and don't even look back because I was what you say incorrigible. I didn't listen to people–people with authority. It's going to be my way or no way at all.

As a child left to his own devices, Patrick Rempkowski sought the help of the Department of Human Resources, which placed him under foster care in several homes. Feeling mistreated by his foster parents, Patrick refused to remain in any of the homes he was assigned to.

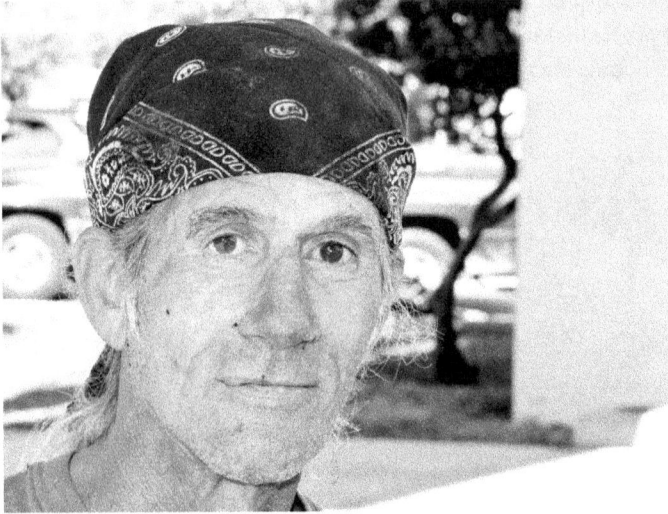

That's why I took off to travel on my own because I wouldn't stay at any of the foster homes they appointed me to. They wanted a slave. They'd go off to their children and go off to the beach and would leave with a mile long list of the things they wanted me to do while they're gone. Mow the lawn. Paint the house.

At age 14, Patrick became a ward of the state and did not require any supervision. Living on his own, he would receive a monthly stipend to cover just enough to pay for food and rent until the age of 18. Before living on the streets, Patrick worked at a pet store in New Brunswick, New Jersey, while sharing an apartment with three other individuals. He began to run into financial difficulties once the pet shop went out of business, and he was forced to find a place of his own for $100 per month and a new job washing dishes at a local restaurant. According to Patrick, his luck soon ran out. Since he had reached the age of 18, the government would no longer provide him with financial assistance. Patrick found himself on the streets soon after being laid off.

I've done everything from clean toilet bowls to build a new house. I hitchhike. I go to truck stops and offer to help them with the load wherever they're going and that's the way I cross country.

Patrick claims not to have refused most work that provided him with income. Like most homeless individuals who find themselves penniless, he must resort to unfavorable means of nourishing himself.

If I don't come up with some odd jobs to make a few bucks during the day, it's called dumpster diving. Go behind the restaurants and go through the dumpster.

Although food service programs and shelters are available to the homeless, many like Patrick choose to avoid them. Becuase of the strict rules imposed on the homeless by these groups, Patrick finds that he would rather get help elsewhere. In fact, he believes these sorts of services provide more obstacles than assistance.

I don't like them. I don't stay in them. I guess it's rules. Have to be in by 10:00. Can't do this and can't do that. It's just like being in jail. If you want to go down there and stay on a line that goes around several different, six blocks, in the nastiest sections of downtown Miami. Sure. Who wants to do that? You can starve to death way before you get up there . . . before you get any food.

Patrick says he is willing to live up to the norms of mainstream society. It seems unfeasible, however, considering all the obstacles a person like him must endure.

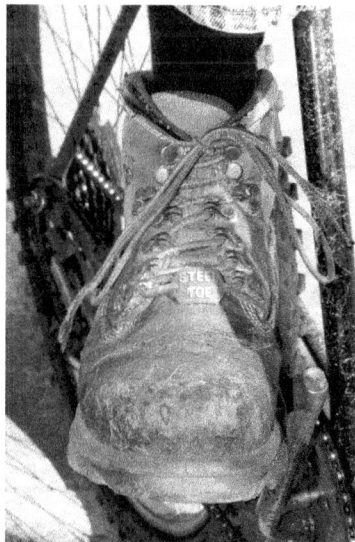

I don't want them to give me nothing. If they could supply us with jobs so that we can pick our own self up off the ground and brush ourselves up, man, and get on with it, everyone would be much better off. They won't give me a job. I'm a three-time convicted felon. I'd be happy having a job to go to every day and my own place to live. I'm very good at carpentry. That would definitely get me on my feet again. I'd be a really happy person. I'd be a happy camper. I sure would.

ANTHONY V. REYNOLDS*

The majority of the people that's homeless on this beach are not drug addicts, they are not alcoholics. They have their issues: family problems, wife/ husband problems, children problems. They just need somebody to talk to. Nobody has the time for them.

---

* Interview conducted by Sabrina F. Sembiante, Miami, Florida, March 30, 2010

Anthony V. Reynolds, now 43, was born in Macon, Georgia and was raised in Belle Glade, Florida. He grew up in what he describes as a pleasant home with loving, caring parents who greatly valued discipline and education. He remembers them encouraging him to do well in school.

They were very strict on education. They always encouraged me, they didn't want me to go in the military, and they wanted me to go to college. I had a scholarship for Boston University, and I didn't go because I'm like, "Aw, man, I'm tired of studying," not knowing when I went in the military, I had to do it anyway. My mom was very dissapointed in me because, you know, I'm very intelligent. I'm very creative, gifted. I sing, I write music, I write plays, I direct, whatever, you know? And that kind of upset her.

In 1985, during his time in the military, Anthony married his current wife who is now living in Texas with his children and grandchildren. He is the father of five daughters, two of whom are from his marriage with his wife. Although they currently live apart, he says that he is still very much in love with her. After having left the military in 1988, Anthony did a fair share of traveling from state to state in order to follow agricultural work and the job opportunities that were available. An event on a job site in 1995 contributed to Anthony's downfall.

I can remember it like it was yesterday. It was in a place called Eustis, Florida, 1995. I was working as a laborer, a truck driver for this guy and we were hauling corn to the packing houses. And we were living in this house, it's a bunch of us. I'm sitting looking at everybody just smoking [crack], I'm like "Man, that must be good," I'm saying to myself. As soon as I said it, this guy heard me. He said "Try it". That was it. And my sister, she's gone now, God bless her soul, she always used to tell me, "Don't never let nobody tell you to try. The first try will keep you going."

Anthony's drug habit caused him to end up living on the streets by 1999. Although he is still in contact with his parents, who live relatively near, they refuse to support him because of his drug addiction. He still struggles to stay clean, citing depression as the number one factor that drives his drug use. He worries for his parents who are now in their late 70s and wishes that he could visit them in Palm Beach County. Although the bus fare to get there is only $6.90, Anthony refuses to beg for money.

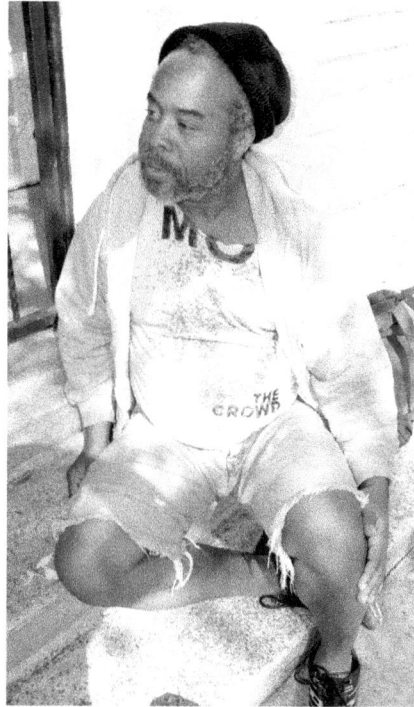

I don't panhandle. Because, you know, it's embarrassing to me. Big, old, strong man like me, "Sir, can you give me $5." It's embarrassing. To some people it's not embarrassing. To me, it is. Eventually, eventually, I'm going to get off the streets.

Anthony also views homelessness in a much different light than many of the other homeless around him. Although his family is asking him to come to Texas, he does not mind living on the streets.

I think it's about choice. I've been in the military. My job kept me out in the woods nine months out of the year, so I'm used to it, you know. I've been prepared for it, so it doesn't bother me. I hear a lot of people that's on the streets, they complain about, "Oh, I'm tired of this," and I look at them like, "You know, here you're getting service checks and you get all this money. Here, I can't even get one."

Although Anthony has tried staying in shelters, he ends up leaving because he feels that the staff is too arrogant and the services are inadequate.

You know, a lot of them have been out here on the streets. Most of them that they're hiring are from the streets or somebody that's recovering from drugs and alcohol. They look at you as if, you know, you're an idiot. You know, "If I did it, you can do it." That kind of mentality. And I can't deal with that. That's a false person. They have a place called the Neighborhood Community Outreach Center which is supposed to assist the homeless by giving them a place to stay. So, if you tell them no, then they figure "Why are you refusing services?" Well I said, "Why don't you dress like me, go into the shelter, stay a month, and then you'll see why nobody wants to go in there." Some of the staff in those places are just butt holes.

Instead, Anthony finds shelter in locations that are covered and quiet. He prefers to avoid being a part of groups of homeless because he doesn't want to be wrongly accused of crimes committed by such groups. Anthony has been arrested before for having an open container of alcohol in public. While he was guilty of the charge, he feels that the justice system is not fair to homeless people.

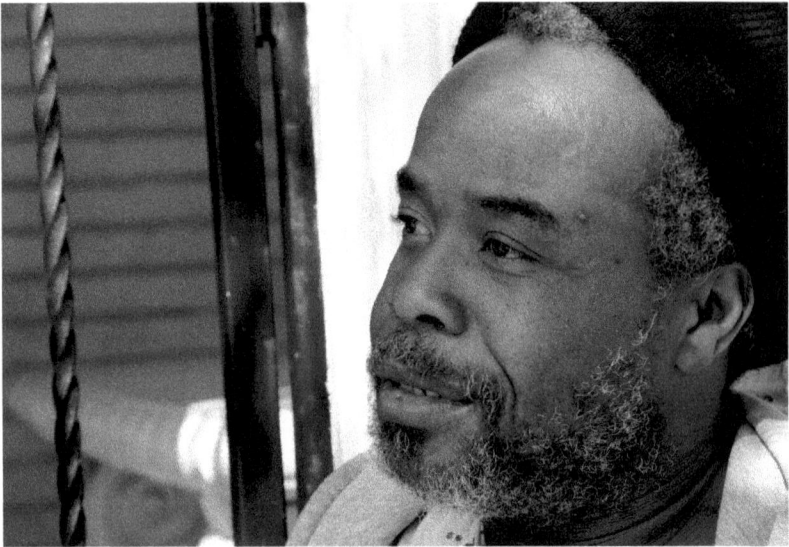

I know how the cops are. They've told me, when there's a crowd of homeless, or anybody, they're going to intervene. Some of them are real nasty. Don't get me wrong. They're very mean. But I've learned to just overlook them. I told one when he arrested me, "Can I share something with you?" I know what the law is because I read it in the library every day. When I was in jail, I was in the law library every day. I said, "I know what the law is. Why would you keep arresting somebody for the same charge and they're just going to throw it out. Why waste taxpayers' money?" Boy, they don't like that. The only thing you get arrested for is [an] open container. What I've asked them is, "Why would you arrest a homeless with an open container when the tourists come here and do whatever the hell they want to do?" Then you get the taxi cabs running around here driving 100 miles an hour, about to kill you, blowing for you to get out the road and it's a red light. They won't answer, they get mad with you. "Oh, you're just being sarcastic." No, no.

Anthony usually gets up in the morning around 4 a.m., prays, meditates, attends church when possible, and spends his days in the public library reading spiritual books. If he could live his life again, he says that he would have chosen to go to college and become what he always wanted to be, a teacher. When asked about his hopes and aspirations for the future, he discusses his goals of becoming a preacher one day.

I read spiritual books, something that encourages me. I don't look for people to encourage me; I try to encourage myself because people will mislead you. My thing is I want to get off the streets, not just to get off for me, but get off to reach back and get those that are still out there. That is a goal that I have. And I'm gonna achieve it, because by me being a veteran, I can apply for a VA loan, and build a house, get a building, a business, or whatever. I mean my heart is for the homeless. I see myself preaching. Just this morning, I could see it clear as day. You know, being able to share my testimony, "Hey, bro, I've been there."

ASHLEY WHITE[*]

The best part of being a mom is you want to do the right thing for your kid. So the best thing I could do is have my grandparents adopt him until I get myself together.

[*] Interview conducted by Eugene F. Provenzo, Jr. and Alain Bengochea, Miami Beach, Florida, April 10, 2010

Ashley White is from Oklahoma City, Oklahoma. She is almost 22 years old. She came to Miami with her fiancé whose family lives in the city. They have nowhere to live, so they sleep on the beach at night. During the day they panhandle to earn money. She has one child who is being raised by her grandparents in Oklahoma, and she is currently four months pregnant.

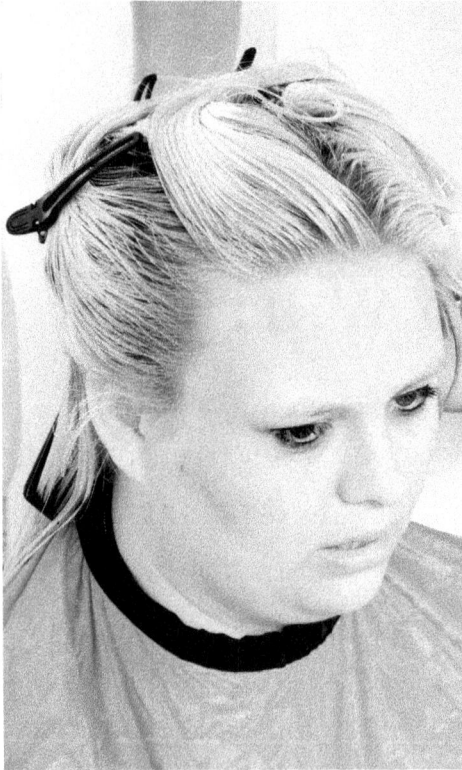

We go to McDonald's almost five times a day. It's harder for me because I'm pregnant. . . Right now I'm taking prenatal vitamins. . . I'm actually a lot healthier than I have been, [compared to] my first pregnancy. My son wasn't as healthy—he has a lot of issues when I was on the streets. I was on drugs for a long time, and I have been clean off for five years. I started when I was fifteen. . . All I do now is smoke cigarettes.

Ashley relinquished custody of her first child to her grandparents when he was 6 months old. She did not want him on the street while she was attempting to restructure her life.

The best part of being a mom is you want to do the right thing for your kid. So the best thing I could do is have my grandparents adopt him until I get myself together.

Ashley recently secured a job doing artificial tattoos. She wants to go back to school and earn her General Education Diploma (GED). She talks about being a social worker, a job she feels she would be particularly qualified to hold because of her own personal experience.

Ever since I was 11, I have been in foster care. I was in group home facilties. . . I want to be able to help someone like people helped me.

Ashley does not get along with her mother, who is an alcoholic. She says that her mother allowed her stepfather to molest her and her other siblings. Ashley complained to the police about her stepfather when she was 11, and he was eventually convicted of child molestation. He is currently serving time in jail for his crime. He has threatened to kill Ashley for having turned him in.

She does not have a relationship with her biological father. Ashley hopes to get an apartment and stay in Miami. Her fiancé starts a job in a hotel soon.

I love Miami. It's gorgeous. It's different. People are a lot nicer than other places. . . In Oklahoma I used to go in stores just to make money, steal clothes and sell them. It was not what I wanted because I knew I could have went to jail. But at the same time, with a lot of things, people would help us out, but they wanted something [in] return. . . Out here it's much easier. Out there, if you are walking around, they are going to arrest you. . . That's how people are out there.

Ashley tries to take advantage of the rescue missions in Miami. She was kicked out of one shelter because she would smoke cigarettes. Living on the street has been a brutal experience for Ashley. She describes having to be careful with whom she associates. In Oklahoma she was raped while living out on the streets. In general she feels safer in Miami than she did in Oklahoma and has no plans to go back. She feels things are looking up for her. Overall coming to Miami has been a good experience for her.

DALE BRANCH[*]

Your depression is rising. And then on top of depression is the recession. So I feel like I'm stuck for good. It looks like this is going to be it. You know they call it a recession, but for people who are marginal, this might as well be a depression.

---

[*] Interview conducted by Sabrina F. Sembiante, Miami, Florida, March 30, 2010

Dale Branch was born in Saint Thomas in the Virgin Islands. He grew up in Charlotte, North Carolina. During his childhood, Dale's family experienced some difficulties, and Dale was sent to live with his aunt, his mother's sister, in New York. She had married a veteran and was living in a house they had bought in the 1960's.

There were some problems—you know, like families have problems? When my mother had problems, she called her sister in New York and said, "Could you take some of your nieces and nephews?" So we moved there.

Dale has lived in Miami since 1970. During this time, he has gone home to the Virgin Islands every 5 or 10 years to visit Saint Thomas. During the 1980's, he attended college. He did not get a chance to finish the program because he took a job in Montego Bay, Jamaica. After having returned to the United States, Dale was able to secure a job working for the Ritz soda company. His salary made it possible for him to live in South Beach for 10 years. He fondly remembers his apartment there.

I had a beautiful apartment. Furnace, kitchen, closet, bathroom. It was like a studio or something-new—$400 a month for 10 years. They never raised it. After about 10 years, they raised the rent like three times as much. The apartment is still there. Every once in a while I take a bus to see it. They renovated it, you know.

When the rent was raised, Dale was no longer able to afford the apartment. He states that he became disoriented and lost his way in terms of finding another place to live. He also didn't know who to turn to. This is when he first started living in shelters.

I'd be homeless for a spell, and then I'd get a little help. I was living in the Salvation Army on 36th street, but it only lasted a couple of months. I was placed in a couple of places, but the places were temporary—two months, three months. It was like a seesaw. The services they provided was real good, but only for three months.

Dale contemplates where he is going to sleep tonight and discusses the challenges and difficulties he has faced during his two years of homelessness. Securing food is another source of stress in Dale's life, and he states that he tries to follow the crowds to find something to eat. When nothing is available, Dale opts to sleep in order to forget his hunger and be able to make it through two or three days without needing nourishment.

In the beginning I was very worried because I was new. It's lonely, it's loud. But after a while, you either find out by yourself, somebody thoughtful tells you, or you ask, "Where's lunch? Where's breakfast? Where's dinner?" Somebody's going to tell you. After a few years, you get to know the area and the people where they congregate. If you've been homeless for a couple of years, you know where you used to talk to people, and see all the people where they hang out. You start to hang out there because we're all in the same boat.

Congregating with other homeless people can be dangerous. Dale recounts an incident with another homeless man that almost got out of control.

Over the years, I've come close to death. Standing in line for chow, it's real easy to get into some conflict, because everybody is anxious just for the meal. And some argument started with a guy next to me. And before you know it, we were at each other. He had ran to the side and picked up a pipe. We were both running in different directions. In the heat of the moment, he ran to one side. I seen him going, picking it up, and before he caught up to me, the people there had done separated us. I also constantly worry about people stealing stuff. That's why I don't keep a lot. All my stuff that I own is in one bag. Two shirts, two pairs of pants, and you know, like shaving, deodorant. I usually sleep with it under my head, so that if they take it, more than likely I will get up. But if you got a lot of stuff, that's the problem.

Dale has had a history of drug use. He remembers first using drugs during his high school and college years. His habit became so bad that at times he did not remember which drugs and how much of them he used. Although Dale tries to abstain from drug use at this point in his life, he says that he turns to it at times in order to make him feel better and forget his troubles.

On the streets, you're depressed. You're trying to feel good. The people around you are feeling good—getting high, smoking, beer, whatever. It's easy to start, it's easy to get addicted. Sometimes you don't know what people cook up. That's why I say sometimes I don't even know what I took. All the popular ones.

One item that Dale keeps with him at all times is a camcorder. He was able to buy it off someone in the streets for $20. He knows that if he didn't take advantage of the offer at the time, he probably would never have a chance to own one. He knows that it is probably not worth a whole lot more than what he paid, but he gets pleasure in taking pictures of the people around him.

I just got it a couple of months ago. RCA, small wonder. I mostly take the people around me because they, like everybody else, they are the perfect subject to photograph. The cutting edge, ground zero. Human life—for me, they are ideal. To take their goings and comings. It's sort of a reflection of what I do.

Dale hopes that his future will bring better circumstances for him. He looks forward to living in a place that is peaceful and happy. He wants to continue living in Miami and would like to live with his family who has never come to the mainland. Most of all, he wants food, clothing, and shelter.

JEROME HENDERSON[*]

I don't take nothing from nobody. . . The only thing I ask is will you help me out.

* Interview conducted by Kristen Doorn, Miami, Florida, March 28, 2010

Jerome Henderson is a Vietnam veteran. He has been in the Miami area for four years. He originally came to South Florida when he returned from the Vietnam War in the early 1970s.

I was in the military. I'm a Vietnam vet. I don't think . . . I don't deserve to be treated like this. Not really.

Although he has received disability payments, it is difficult for him to survive on this income. And because of his disabilities, it is almost impossible for him to get a steady job and make a living.

I'm blind in one eye. I can't see out of the other. I try to medicate myself. I got a bad leg, you know.

He openly expresses his frustration with the Miami Police Department. He was arrested by the police during the week prior to this interview. They accused him of staying in a "no-trespassing" area in a neighborhood that he understood to be a "safe zone." "Safe zones" for the homeless are areas near health clinics, soup kitchens, and other services, where they cannot be arrested or picked up for temporarily sleeping. Like other homeless individuals, Jerome feels that the police treat him unfairly, and simply want to keep him marginalized. But he considers the streets to be his home and believes that he has a right to stay in the city, just like any other citizen. As a result, Jerome is forced to stay mobile, moving from place to place, in search of a safe area to serve as his temporary residence.

They want to run off the homeless and build this community. It ain't no community. It's just an island-an accident waiting to happen . . . They [the Miami Police Department] are targeting me because I'm hungry.

Like many other homeless individuals in the Miami area, Jerome prefers not to stay in the shelters within the city. Many of these shelters are extremely overcrowded. In addition, rules and regulations within these establishments tend to remain very strict for the homeless, which is often difficult for the individuals who utilize these shelters regularly.

No, too much congestion [in the shelters]. They think they own them. 'Cause they off the streets and then because you off the street, you got more seniority than anybody else.

So Jerome stays on the move, sticking together with other homeless individuals, looking for the next "safe zone" to call home for the night.

JOSEPH SHEPHARD[*]

They discard us like a bunch of cattle. They herd us around. Whenever they have an election here or whenever they have a big event here, like the arts festival, they sweep us, like a gigantic street sweeper.

---

* Interview conducted by Ryan W. Pontier, Miami, Florida, March 28, 2010

Joseph Shephard, referred to as Shephard on the street, resided in a house for 55 years before becoming homeless. He was adopted at a young age but lived in what he describes as a warm house with a mother and father. In addition to Shephard, his mother cared for several other children. They continue to play an important role in his life.

I've been always at a house for 55 years. I always had a place. I had money. I had everything I needed. He [pointing to a friend] used to live with me at my house with my mom. My mom took in 16 kids and put them all in the living room. She put them all in sleeping bags. She spent her whole check on sleeping bags for all those kids. And it makes me cry right now. You know what I mean? My mother was a saint. She adopted me from 2 years old. I never knew my [birth] mother.

In the course of only one year, Shephard lost several members of his inner circle.

I lost my mother, my father, my brother in one year. And then I had a good friend that was needing back surgery, so I paid $20,000 for a friend of mine to have a back surgery in Lee County, Fort Myers, and he died during surgery. So I lost my best friend after all that, and my money.

To his surprise, Shephard learned that his parents had a reverse mortgage on the house, a debt he simply could not afford to pay after having been so generous with his friend.

They had a reverse mortgage on the house, and I didn't know it, and they foreclosed on me. My mother and father bought that house in 1946, and it was . . . they bought it for $7,000, 1946. They sold it . . . they finally sold it to Wells Fargo, which had the reverse mortgage, sold it for $275,000. I didn't get but 30 grand out of it. Thirty grand. So I got my arms ripped off, my heart ripped off when my mother died, and then they broke my spine when they took my house.

And here I am.

Shephard worked in the carpenters' union for 30 years. His job took him to several army bases throughout the country. Despite his time with the union, he has had difficulty obtaining his pension. According to Shephard, the union owes him $60,000.

What I do is I work with metal. I do everything a carpenter does, but I do it all with metal—tie it, screw it, weld it, whatever. And I work[ed] 30 years. They owe me $60,000. And they only wanna pay me 27 grand.

The lack of access to money or any solid way of obtaining an income compounds Shephard's situation on the street. He has the added responsibility of caring for a dog, a loyal pet of 14 years. Shephard is constantly retreating from the police, who, he claims, incessantly usher him and all other homeless people away from the public eye, especially during big events in the city.

They discard us like a bunch of cattle. They herd us around. Whenever they have an election here or whenever they have a big event here, like the arts festival, they sweep us, like a gigantic street sweeper. The cops do. And they always use that right there, my dog. It's not his fault he's here. And he doesn't do nothing but sleep.

They said, "Either, Shephard, you do what we tell you to do. You either go over there, you go over there, or you stay the fuck away, out of sight." Out of sight, out of mind. That's what they always say. "Stay the fuck out of sight. We won't bother you and your dog." They always use the dog, 'cause they know this is my love. Fourteen years I've been with him.

Shephard creates the following analogy when expressing his feelings on being homeless.

We're like . . . back hundreds of years ago, they had people who had leprosy, right? Ok, they always stayed in caves, and in their little shelters, and nobody fucked with them, right? And that's just how I kind of feel . . . they kind of treat us the same kind of way out here.

Despite these difficulties on the street, Shephard is a father figure, both literally and figuratively. He has three biological sons, ranging in age from 19 to 31, and approximately 35 adopted children from the street. Shephard says that he has always cared for people, and they have always sought refuge with him.

I got like 35, 40 kids. All kids off the street. And I got my three blood sons. That was probably the best thing I did in my whole entire life. I delivered every one of them. Right in the room. . . . when I was living at the house, we kept bringing in kids that were homeless, kids that were in gangs, kids that were doing the wrong thing . . . I got like a . . . a following. I got like a . . . they flock to me. They always have. Ever since I was a kid, bro. I don't know what it is. I had a good rapport with people.

They feel comfortable with me, and they know they are, because I'll take care of them. And they'll take care of me. They're like family, bro.

Shephard will continue to fight to live on the streets of Miami. He is aware what he is up against. He knows the attitudes, he knows the people, and he knows the abuse. All have been an everyday reality for him.

I've been through the gangs, I've been through the drug scene, I've been through . . . first I started with Woodstock. Okay, 1969 I started with drugs. I did drugs . . . I got a scar all the way up and down my arm from shootin' up cocaine for 25 years. I ain't touched it in 10 years. I don't do any drugs. All I do is drink a little bit of this [beer], and that's all I do. I kicked everything out here.

My worst enemy [is] living out here on the street. It's devastating. It's mental and physical torture. That's what this is.

Hopefully Shephard's "family" will be enough to help him endure life on the streets.

Note: Kimberly requested that her photograph not be used with her interview since she is afraid of being found by people who may wish to harm her.

KIMBERLY JONES*

On a daily basis, I pray how to get money. I get my food stamps and I survive through that. But on a daily basis, praying gets my money.

* Interview conducted by Kristen Doorn, Miami, Florida, March 28, 2010

She goes by Kimberly Jones, or Kim, because she does not want anyone to know her real name. She has only been homeless for a few months, after losing the house in which she lived.

I've been on the streets three months totally. I had lost my house three months ago, through my ex-boyfriend.

She is gracious and open to discussing her story and opinions. It is evident from her responses, however, that she already feels the effects of the tough environment in which she is forced to live each day as a homeless individual, even after such a short period of time.

You can't stay around here because like, it's like, it's dangerous, for one. The cops, they harass us. . . . I feel like we should all be treated equally. It's depressing, you know. . . . And I feel like that's not a good . . . that's not a good idea for them. You know what I mean? Because I feel we [deserve] equal right[s]. We here, we fight for our own rights, our civil rights. I think we should all be treated equally. It don't matter about the color. We all share the same blood. I just feel they [the police] should help us out. To put us into a shelter, they should help us out here. You know what I mean? If they see us begging, they should say, "Hey, would you guys like to be into a shelter or something?"

Kimberly, like many other homeless individuals, feels the constant pressure of the police—the discrimination and harassment. She feels a constant need to be on the move and to be looking for the next place to stay.

It's my pleasure that you guys come by to talk to us. Because, you know, like the cops here, it's like they're here. They here daily. The only thing they do is harass us. And I really appreciate that you guys come around us. You guys give out cards and whatever. It's a blessing, you know, because we don't get that from people that be scared to come around us. And we get harassed daily. It is trouble out here you know.

Kimberly is always looking for ways to make money and to support herself. Prior to living in Miami, she attended a culinary arts school in Los Angeles. After moving to Miami, she worked with a catering company but was laid off after a year and a half.

I also find some work around here. Like, I help out. Like, tonight, I helped this church out, called the Lighthouse. I helped them out. I cooked for them. And they give me a opportunity to be the first one to pick what I want, like clothes, soap, deodorant. I be the first one to get that. They are a real help for me, you know what I mean . . . [Sometimes] I braid hair. I don't ask them for nothing. When they give it to me, I just do hair, you know.

Like many other homeless individuals, she remains ambitious. She would like to return to work and find a new home someday. In the meantime, however, she does whatever she can to make it, day by day.

On a daily basis, I pray how to get money. I get my food stamps and I survive through that. But, on a daily basis, praying gets my money.

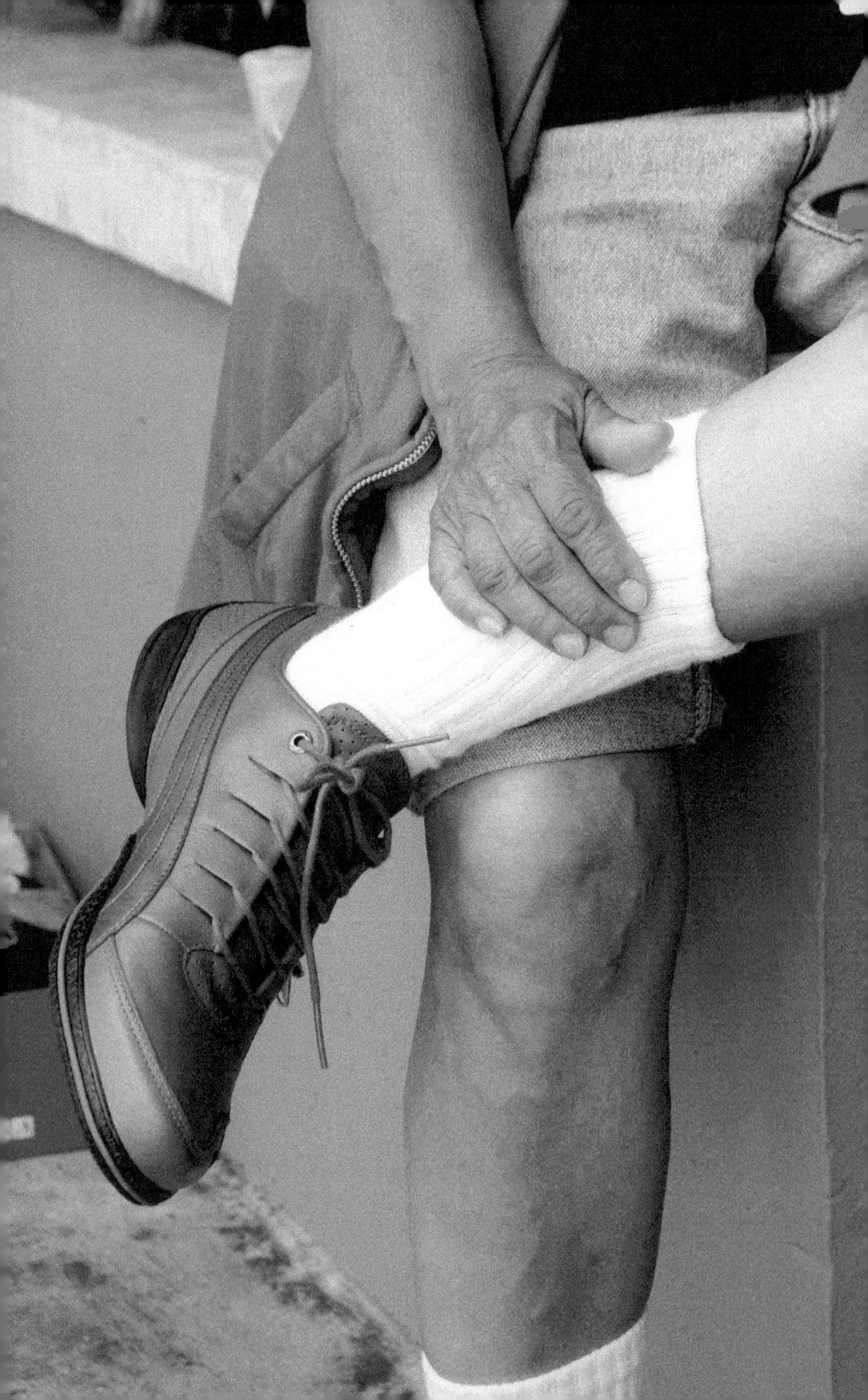

MS. RED*

I know I'm going to make it. I can see it.

---

* Interview conducted by Alain Bengochea, Miami, Florida, March 28, 2010

When asked to choose between two options—returning to her old way of life with a fixed income and a place to call home or remaining among the homeless—Ms. Red's preference would be to live on the streets. This, however, was not always the case. At age 64, Ms. Red never expected to become homeless in the latter decades of her life. Arriving in Miami under extraordinary circumstances, she made a life-altering decision in a time of despair. Ms. Red conceals her name as she does most aspects of her life, hoping to remain undiscovered. The reason for much of her distress is attributed to her husband, a man whom she claims chased her out of her home state.

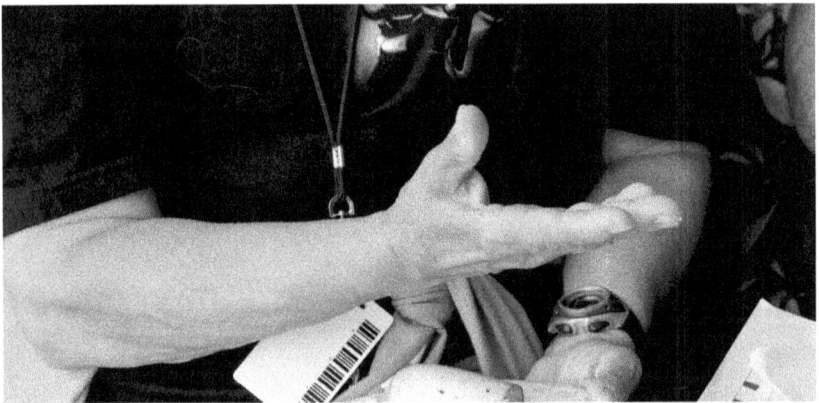

I know him since I was 16 and we had other marriages. He thought it was going to be okay to say that he was never going to gamble when he's with me, and he married me. Since 1980 . . . kept leaving and kept leaving. Kept bothering me and kept bothering. What happened was, he can't treat me. . . . He's a gambler. When they lose, they go ballistic. And he gambled and we were fighting like animals. Fighting, fighting, fighting . . . When they lose, they go crazy. I believe, in some ways, he was bipolar, you know, because one minute he loves me, and the next minute he wants to gamble. And then right away he wants to kill everyone he knew. I can't live like that.

The conflict in her marriage had far-reaching consequences. It affected her well-being, employment, and relationships with the people surrounding her. Trying to avoid her husband at all costs was an impossible feat while living in the same city. Ms. Red felt compelled to leave her life in New York when her husband became a danger to those around her at the job she held in a newspaper advertising agency.

He threatened them, that if I kept working there he would blow the place up. And they wanted to call 911, and I said, "No, I'll just go," 'cause the girls were frightened. At this point, they were afraid. And once he knows where I work, he would come there. So what's the use? So my girlfriend said, "Let's go to Florida." I just, "Yeah, let's go. Let's go." I don't ever want to go back to New York.

Expecting to find comfort from those she knew, Ms. Red moved to Florida with friends she had known for 45 years. Unfortunately, her expectations to leave a life filled with heartache would not be achieved. As a self-taught artist, she worked for her friends who employed her as a painter in many of the restaurants they owned. Ms. Red would design elaborate murals in order to increase the value of the restaurants intended for resale. She also tended to the household duties as a form of payment for her living situation.

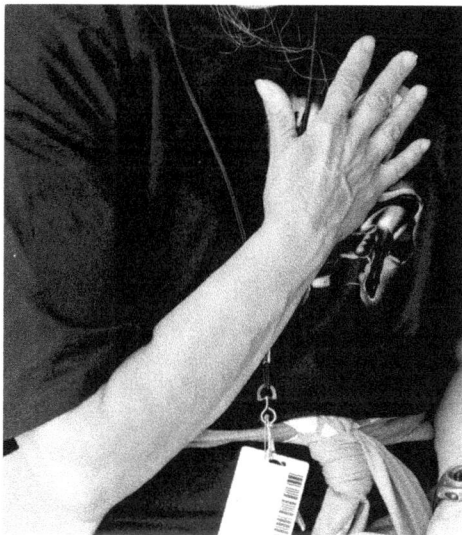

Well, my whole life I've been doing murals in New York. They were able to sell restaurants for so much extra money because they did these humongous, gigantic, beautiful murals. Some were Greek. I did some for Israeli[s]. But they kept taking all of my money. You can't go to a place . . . You have to have rent and security. I had it! But they knew the situation I was in, so they took my Social Security plan, and they took my food stamps.

Even though she has made significant strides, Ms. Red never imagined that she would have such trouble in getting the help she would need to regain her independence. Fortunately, she was able to find one individual who voiced his concern—a stranger on the street.

They finally gave me the key because most of the time I was in the house. If I left the house, I couldn't get back in unless they... Well, they gave me the key. And I walked outside because I was contemplating suicide. I said, "I don't want to live like this anymore." And about a block away, I met this fellow, black fellow on a bicycle. He said, "Lady, you look like you're in trouble." And I said, "Yeah." And he took me to all these places to show me where to eat and what to do. Like an angel. How did he know that I was in trouble? And here I am.

Upon meeting this stranger, Ms. Red sought out the resources available to those in need within the Miami community. On this visit to the First United Methodist Church, which traditionally provides support to the homeless, she managed to get free medical advice for her psoriasis from one of the physicians. She received a new pair of red sneakers, which she fawned over. One can usually find Ms. Red at Camillus House, which is now the place she calls home. It is also where she feels most safe.

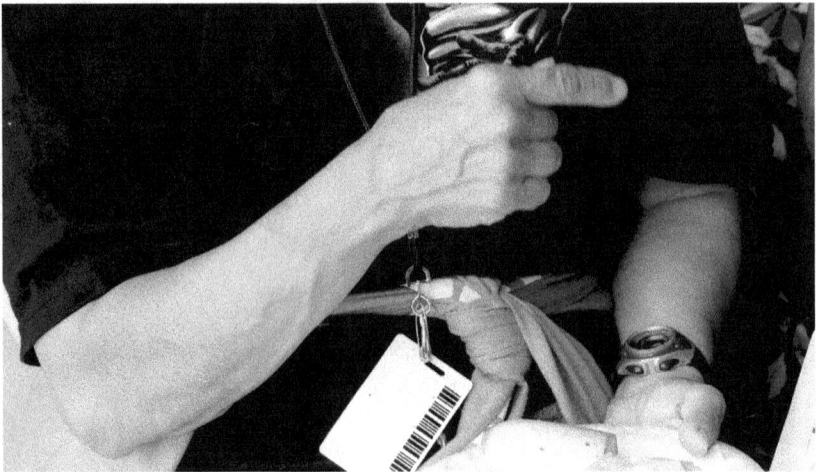

And I'm happier than I was before, yeah. Sleeping on the floor on a mat. And things are not great, but I don't feel threatened and I don't feel suicidal anymore. Just got a pair of brand new sneakers. Got my feet done. I look at the bright side of things, and I think they're going to find me a place that I can . . . Because I'm not a drug addict, and I'm not an alcoholic. I'm just in a bad spot.

The discomfort of living in a homeless shelter is a small price to pay for the sense of freedom she now experiences. Although she is not entirely adjusted to life as a homeless individual, Ms. Red remains positive and has found ways to deal with the unfavorable conditions.

One of the most horrendous things that happen is the bathroom. It's gross. Women are gross. No, really. You can go in a men's room and maybe they pee on the seat or put the seat up. Wow. Women are gross. Disgusting. I don't know where they were brought up. Or maybe they were born on the street. I don't know. And then there's so many of us in one bathroom. So as soon as you get there, they're knocking on the door. Not only can you not go when you want to go, but if you want to go, you have to . . . So I go everywhere else.

Trying to become self-sufficient once again, Ms. Red has made frequent visits to a social worker. With this assistance, she hopes to once again possess the necessary documents that would enable her to work, which she lost while living on the street. Despite the fact that she is facing long delays in the process, she believes that she will eventually find employment.

My social worker was supposed to do the paperwork so I won't have to have originals. She made five or six appointments, and broke them. So I got upset about that. I said, how professional this is, you know? If I had been on drugs, I would have understood that, and then I'm not on drugs . . . I'm afraid of pills and all that stuff. But I didn't. But that's very, very bad for people. She's doing this to a lot of people, and they're all complaining.

Ms. Red describes her current life as living in paradise. Having forged meaningful relationships with other homeless individuals, she feels fulfillment in her life.

Since I'm here, I met better people than I've ever met in my life. I've met five or six girls that treat me better than their children. And some of the men too. They shiver over me. They give me blankets. They [say] . . . "Mommy, you've got to eat. And here's an extra coffee. Come with us." I've met the best people in my life. We're not talking about the crazy ones. We're not talking about the nut jobs. The ones that talk to themselves and all . . . When I thought I was going to leave one day, I cried. 'Cause I want these people to be with me the rest of my life.

Envisioning herself years down the line, she wants to share her life with her newfound friends, but in a different setting. She feels she could realize these dreams when she once again has an apartment and a stable job. This, she hopes, would ultimately provide her peace of mind and security.

MARGO KENYON[*]

I think there is protection in numbers, especially being women.

[*] Interview with Eugene F. Provenzo, Jr., Miami Beach, Florida, April 22, 2010

Margo Kenyon was born in West Viriginia and is 38 years old. She has lived in Miami for nine years. She came to the area to particpate in a drug rehabilitation program, having been addicted to cocaine. She has also had issues with alcohol abuse. She has been clean for a month. She has been featured as a nude model in over 30 men's magazines and has been an actor in roughly the same number of adult films. She lives on the street with Bobbie Olson (see page 35) and spends some time with a boyfriend who is a professional and lives in a luxury condominium on Miami Beach. She explains that she and Bobbie look out for each other.

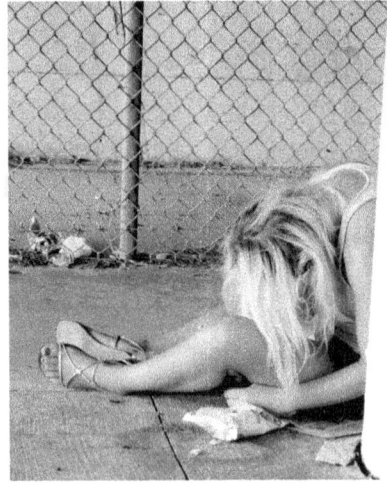

Whatever we have we share. If she has something, she gives me half. If I have something, I give her half. . . . I think there is protection in numbers, especially being women.

Margo feels it is important to project confidence on the street and not let people feel she is a victim or is weak. She does not like staying at shelters.

I did that one night and I'll never do it again. It's insane. You go there at 3:00 in the afternoon. You wait out there two hours, getting a number. Then they bring you in and you do a little cleaning. Then they throw you in a little room where you have 10 people waiting to take a shower, and then they throw you out at 5:00 in the morning. . . . Whatever belongings you have, you have to haul them along with you.

Margo claims she has had most of her personal possessions picked up by the Homeless Assistance Center. She would love to have a secure locker to keep her things in. Many people on the street come to her for help. She feels that some of the police deliberately harass homeless people, while others watch out for them and try to protect them. In her opinion, many people on the street need help with drug addiction. Unless they get effective treatment, they will continue to stay out on the street. She feels that detox programs are not effective, since "they make you sick."

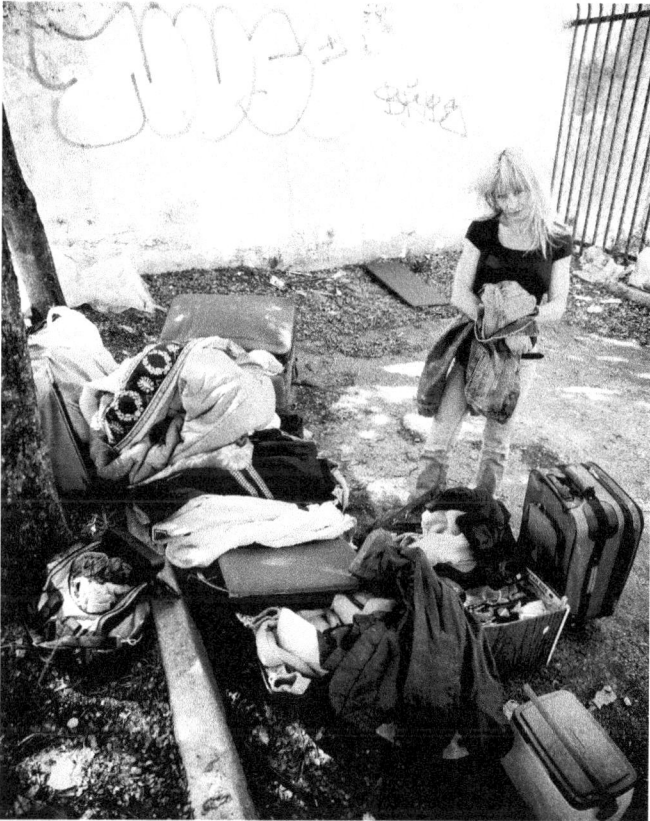

AFTERWORD

Homelessness is a problem that affects many people in America. It is usually the result of an interplay of multifaceted, complex circumstances that forces individuals to choose between critical life essentials, such as food, shelter, and other basic needs. Until we, as a society, are able to end homelessness, it is important that our towns and cities, as well as state and federal governments, continue to enact policy changes that will aid the homeless individuals that make up such an important sector of our society. The National Alliance to End Homelessness is a nonprofit, non-partisan organization committed to the effort of eliminating homelessness in the United States. Started in 1983 by a group of concerned leaders who joined together and collaborated in order to help meet the emergency needs of a growing population of homeless individuals, the Alliance has grown significantly in terms of its efforts, with the help of federal leadership and local activism. In fact, between 2005 and 2007, the Alliance assisted in decreasing the homelessness population by 10 percent with the help of changes in federal and local policy, improved education of the general public and policymakers, as well as expanded efforts within communities to implement best practices (National Alliance to End Homelessness, 2009).

The Alliance offers a number of resources that provide integral information on federal policies that affect homeless populations throughout the nation. One of the most important policy pieces that the organization produces is its policy guide. This guide provides pertinent information on the most important federal programs, policies, and legislation affecting homelessness. The 2009 Policy Guide applies the principles set forth in the "Ten Year Plan to End Homelessness" to legislation currently before Congress. There are two types of legislation that Congress uses to create Federal policy. On a yearly basis, Congress passes appropriations setting funding levels for Federal programs. Many of these appropriations are designated to aid poor and homeless people. In addition, Congress works to authorize legislation to initiate or reform programs and to influence the economic environment through tax policy and additional regulations (National Alliance to End Homelessness, 2009).

With the inauguration of President Barack Obama in 2009, a change in leadership resulted within the Federal government. The Federal administrative offices have developed new policies on housing and homelessness, some of which are already in action (National Alliance to End Homelessness, 2009). With the passing of the $800 billion stimulus package in 2009, aimed at assisting the country in its economic recovery, the Homelessness Prevention and Rapid Re-Housing Program (HPRP) began giving out funds that they anticipate will help as many as 600,000 Americans avoid homelessness. These funds provide aid to individuals who are trying to pay security deposits, utility bills, moving bills, and rent checks. This assistance helps them avoid the process of eviction or often assists them in moving from transitional housing into their own apartments. The assistance lasts from 3 to 18 months (National Health Care for the Homeless Council, 2009).

Since the beginning of 2010, additional measures have been enacted by the Federal government that continue to affect and assist homeless individuals. On March 23, 2010, the President signed into law new federal health reform legislation that aims to extend health care insurance coverage to 32 million Americans (who are currently uninsured) by the year 2019. As a part of this legislation, Medicaid expansion planned in 2014 will cover 16 million new enrollees. Areas of particular importance to people who are homeless are as follows: a) an expansion of Medicaid to everyone at or below 133 percent of the Federal Poverty Level (FPL) without any categorical restrictions; b) an investment of $11 billion over five years for the Community Health Center Programming; c) an investment of $1.5 billion over five years for the National Health Service Corps; d) efforts to target the shortage of nurses by implementing incentives and a career path for nursing; e) efforts to increase the supply of primary care providers; as well as f) efforts to support the development of training programs that focus on primary care models (National Health Care for the Homeless Council, 2009). Congress has also been working on additional pieces of housing legislation that will aid homeless individuals, including a landmark housing bill that was passed in the summer of 2009. This bill was used to create the National Housing Trust Fund. Additionally, in May 2009, they reauthorized HUD's McKinney-Vento homeless-assistance programs for the first time in almost 20 years (National Alliance to End Homelessness, 2009).

While developing and enacting policy efforts addressing the needs of the homeless are critical at the national level, setting them in place at the local level is equally important. Based on the insights we obtained from this study, we would like to suggest that the following policy recommendations be considered for enactment in Miami. We propose policy at two levels: 1. Basic Recommendations and 2. Experiments and Innovations Worth Considering.

Policy Recommendations Addressing Homelessness in Miami

Our research on the conditions of the homeless in Miami suggest to us a number of specific policy recommendations. Our suggestions are drawn from the wide range of people we talked to for the interviews included in this book. They are not necessarily new, but nonetheless we think that they are worth considering. In addition, we would like to suggest projects and activities that would be worthy of consideration.

Basic Recommendations:

1. Basic healthcare and emergency services should be made more available in the neighborhoods in Miami where the homeless tend to populate. Currently, for the downtown Miami population, Jackson Memorial Hospital is the primary site where homeless populations go in an emergency. Mobile and storefront clinics in selected sites could significantly facilitate the receipt of better treatment and long-term care for homeless populations.
2. Drug treatment should be made more easily available. Methadone treatment, for example, is costly and not always easy to receive. Clinic hours and locations do not necessarily meet the needs of dependent people living on the streets. New ways of providing services, including mobile services and clinics, need to be considered. In addition, transportation to clinic sites need to be made more practical from the neighborhoods where homeless populations are primarily located.
3. Increasing the public's awareness of why homelessness exists in a place like Miami and that there are a wide range of causes for homelessness (ranging from economic and legal issues, to psychological and social problems to drug and alcohol dependency). In addition, it needs to be recognized that a certain number of people choose street life because they like its freedom compared to more traditional models of habitation and living.
4. In recognition of the preference to remain out of shelters, service providers should offer programs and housing that allow the homeless to live with fewer restrictions and can support their gradual move into more permanent housing by tolerating "mistakes."
5. Shelters need to be expanded. Currently the available sites are overcrowded, leading to many people deciding that the street is a more comfortable and safer place to be.

6. More affordable housing needs to be made available in Miami for people with lower levels of income. The average salary in Miami in 2008 was just under $29,000; spending 30% of one's income on housing means that the average worker cannot afford anything more than $700 in rent. Many people earn far below the average in a city that rents apartments for well above an affordable cost.

7. Homeless individuals need to be made more aware of the potential services that are available to them and how to access these services.

8. Provisions need to be made for greater systematic job training and job opportunities for homeless populations, particularly for jobs with living wages.For teens and young adults who are homeless, there needs to be a better continuum of care that creates "open -door" opportunities at various access points in the provider system. Young people face a somewhat different set of circumstances, with fewer services available to unaccompanied young people with no family to fall back on.

9. Prevention of homelessness is cost effective, however, money generally tends to fall on the side of intervention. Practices that can sustain individuals and help families remain in their homes means that fewer problems will become compounded by hardships faced on the streets.

Experiments and Innovations Worth Considering:

1. The creation of more safe zones for homeless populations in Miami. These could be in public parks, designated areas near police stations, underlying selected sections of the downtown overpass system in downtown Miami, etc. The creation of safe public sleeping areas that are clean with readily available bathroom and shower facilities, secure lockers, laundry facilites and healthcare and feeding programs would be an important contribution. While many of these services are provided by groups such as Camillus House and the Homeless Assistance Center (HAC), we feel it would be worthwhile to have opportunities for homeless individuals that are less institutional in nature.

2. Greater opportunities need to be provided for "starting over." These would involve expunging of questionable arrest records and criminal sentences.

3. Homeless Prevention/Resource Centers should be established around the county and staffed by workers or volunteers for ex-

tended hours. These would offer people the opportunity to receive a comprehensive needs assessment and be linked up to various services and empowerment opportunities to prevent or end homelessness.

4. Consider the possibility of "wet" shelters (ones that allow some drug and alcohol use) for the purpose of harm reduction amongst homeless individuals who cannot control their substance habits.

5. Provide more support and training to homeless people in advocating for themselves.

6. Given the large number of undocumented immigrants in places like Miami, it is important that we educate these individuals about their basic rights, and concurrently lobby to expand them in local and state legislature. Many are afraid to seek social services or find dead ends due to language and cultural barriers.

7. Put a time-limited moratorium on foreclosures on single-family homes with children present.

Sources

National Alliance to End Homelessness (2009). National alliance to end homelessness: Policy. Retrieved April 12, 2010, from http://www.endhomelessness.org/section/policy

National Health Care for the Homeless Council (2009). Health Care for the Homeless and Health Reform. Retrieved April 12, 2010, from http://www.nhchc.org/KeyHealthReformProvisions.pdf

BIBLIOGRAPHY

The following bibliography provides a selection of key publications on homelessness. For a more comprehensive list see "Appendix 5: Master Bibliography of Publications on Homelessness" in David Levinson, editor, *Encyclopedia of Homelessness*, Vol. 2, Sage Publications: Thousand Oaks, CA, 2004.

America's libraries and the homeless. (n.d.). American Library Association Fact Sheet. Retrieved April 27, 2010, from http://www.ala.org

Anderson, N. (1998). *On hobos and homelessness.* Chicago: University of Chicago Press.

Bahr, H. M. (1973). *Skid row: An introduction to disaffiliation.* New York: Oxford University Press.

Bahr, H. M. (Ed.). (1970). *Disaffiliated man: Essays and bibliography on skid row.* Toronto, Canada: University of Toronto Press.

Baker, S. G. (1994). Gender, ethnicity, and homelessness: accounting for demographic diversity on the streets. *American Behavioral Scientist, 37* (4), 476-504.

Barrow, S., & Lovell, A. M. (1987). Homelessness and the limited options of older women. *Association for Anthropology and Gerontology Newsletter, 8* (4), 3-5.

Barrow, S. M., & Zimmer, R. (1999). Transitional housing and services: A synthesis. In L. B. Fosburg & D. L. Dennis (Eds.), *Practical lessons: The 1998 National Symposium on Homelessness Research* (pp. 10-1-10-31). Washington, D.C.: U.S. Department of Housing and Urban Development and U. S. Department of Health and Human Services.

Bassuk, E. L., & Weinreb, L. (1993). Homeless pregnant women: Two generations at risk. *American Journal of Orthopsychiatry, 63* (3), 348-357.

Baum, A., & Burnes, D. (1993). *A nation in denial: The truth about homelessness.* Boulder, CO: Westview Press.

Baumohl, J. (1989). Alcohol, homelessness, and public policy. *Contemporary Drug Problems, 16,* 281-300.

Baumohl, J. (Ed.). (2003). *Homelessness in America.* Phoenix, AZ: Oryx Press.

Baumohl, J., & Huebner, R. (1991). Alcohol and other drug problems among the homeless. *Housing Policy Debate, 2*, 837-865.

Blasi, G. (1994). And we are not seen: Ideological and political barriers to understanding homelessness. *American Behavioral Scientist, 37*, 563-586.

Blasi, G. L. (1990). Social policy and social science research on homelessness. *Journal of Social Issues, 46* (4), 207-219.

Blau, J. (1992). *The visible poor: Homelessness in the United States.* New York: Oxford University Press.

Bluestone, B., & Harrison, B. (1982). *The deindustrialization of America: Plant closings, community abandonment, and the dismantling of basic industry.* New York: Basic Books.

Breakey, W. R. (1987). Treating the homeless. *Alcohol Health & Research World, 11,* 42-47.

Brickner, E. (Ed.). (1990). *Under the safety net: The health and social welfare of the homeless in the United States.* New York: W. W. Norton.

Bunis, W. K., Yancik, A., & Snow, D. A. (1996). The cultural patterning of sympathy toward the homeless and other victims of misfortune. *Social Problems, 43,* 387-402.

Burt, M. R., Aron, L. Y., Douglas, T., Valente, J., Lee, E., & Iwen, B. (1999). *Homelessness: Programs and the people they serve.* Interagency Council on the Homeless. Retrieved April 27, 2010, from http://www.huduser.org/portal/publications/homeless/homelessness/contents.html

Calsyn, R, & Morse, G. (1992). Predicting psychiatric symptoms among homeless people. *Community Mental Health Journal, 28* (5), 385-395.

Calsyn, R. J., & Morse, G. A. (1990). Homeless men and women: Commonalities and service gender gap. *American Journal of Community Psychology, 18,* 597-608.

Coalition for the Homeless. (2003). *Basic facts about homelessness.* Retrieved April 27, 2010, from http://www.coalitionforthehomeless.org/pages/basic-facts#FACTS

Dolbeare, C. N. (1996). *Homelessness in America.* Phoenix, AZ: Oryx.

Farrow, J. A., Deisher, R. W., Brown, R., Kulig, J. W., & Kipke, M. D. (1992). Health and health needs of homeless and runaway youth. *Journal of Adolescent Health, 13,* 717-726.

Furtado, C. (2002, December 23). For homeless, the Internet is a link to jobs and loved ones. *Miami Herald,* p. 1-A.

Gamache, G., Rosenheck, R. A., & Tessler, R. (2001). The proportion of veterans among homeless men: A decade later. *Social Psychiatry and Psychiatric Epidemiology, 36* (10), 481-485.

Glasser, I., & Bridgman, R. (1999). *Braving the street: The anthropology of homelessness.* New York: Berghahn Books.

Goering, E., Tolomiczenko, G., Sheldon, T., Boydell, K., & Wasylenki, D. (2002). Characteristics of persons who are homeless for the first time. *Psychiatric Services, 53 (11),* 1472-1474.

Gonzalez, G., & Rosenheck, R. A. (2002). Outcomes and service use among homeless persons with serious mental illness and substance abuse. *Psychiatric Services, 53* (4), 437-446.

Herman, D. B., & Susser, E. S. (1998). *Homelessness in America: A collection of articles from the American Journal of Public Health.* Washington, DC: American Public Health Association.

Jencks, C. (1994). *The homeless.* Cambridge, MA: Harvard University Press.

Jones, J. M., Levine, I. S., & Rosenberg, A. (Eds.). (1991). Special issue on homelessness. *American Psychologist, 46,* 1109-1111.

Lee, B. A., & Farrell, C. R. (2003). Buddy, can you spare a dime? Homelessness, panhandling, and the public. *Urban Affairs Review, 38* (3), 299-324.

Lee, B. A., Jones, S. H., & Lewis, D. W. (1990). Public beliefs about the causes of homelessness. *Social Forces, 69* (1), 253-265.

Marcuse, P. (1987, April 4). Why are they homeless? *The Nation, 244 (13).*

Morton, M. (1995). *The tunnel: The underground homeless of New York City.* New Haven, CT: Yale University Press.

Rice, S. A. (1918). The homeless. *Annals of the American Academy of Political Science, 77,* 140-153.

Rossi, E H. (1988). Minorities and homelessness. In G. D. Sandefur & M. Tienda (Eds.), *Divided opportunities: Minorities, poverty, and social policy* (pp. 87-115). New York: Plenum.

Rossi, E H., Wright, J. D., Fisher, G. A., & Willis, G. (1987). The urban homeless: Estimating composition and size. *Science, 235,* 1336-1341.

Rowe, M, (1999). *Crossing the border: Encounters between homeless people and outreach workers.* Berkeley and Los Angeles: University of California Press.

Rowe, M., Hoge, M. A., & Fisk, D. (1998). Services for mentally ill homeless persons: Street-level integration. *American Journal of Orthopsychiatry,*68(3), 490-496.

Rowe, M., Hoge, M. A., & Fisk, D. (1996). Critical issues in serving people who are homeless and mentally ill. *Administration and Policy in Mental Health, 23,* 555-565.

Schumacher, J. E., Mennemeyer, S. T., Milby, J. B., Wallace, D., & Nolan, K. (2002). Costs and effectiveness of substance abuse treatments for homeless persons. *Journal of Mental Health Policy and Economics, 5*(1), 33-42.

Shuman, B. A. (1996). Down and out in the reading room: The homeless in the public library. In B. McNeil & D. J. Johnson (Eds.), *Patron behavior in libraries: A handbook of positive approaches to negative situations* (pp. 3-17). Chicago: American Library Association.

Silver, J. (1996, Winter). Libraries and the homeless: Caregivers or enforcers. *The Katharine Sharp Review, No. 2.* Retrieved April 27, 2010 from http://alexia.lis.uiuc.edu

Simmons, R.C. (1985, Fall). The homeless in the public library: Implications for access to libraries. *Reference Quarterly, 25,* 110-120.

Smith, A., & Smith, D. (2001). *Emergency and transitional shelter population: 2000.* Washington DC: U.S. Government Printing Office.

Smollar, J. (1999). Homeless youth in the United States: Description and developmental issues. In M. Raffaelli & R. W. Larson (Eds.), *New Directions for Child and Adolescent Development, 85,* 47-58. San Francisco: Jossey-Bass.

Snow, D., Anderson, L., & Koegel, P. (1994). Distorting tendencies in research on the homeless. *American Behavioral Scientist, 37,* 461-475.

Snow, D. A., & Anderson, L. (1987). Identity work among the homeless: The verbal construction and avowal of personal identities. *American Journal of Sociology, 92,* 1336-1371.

Snow, D. A., & Anderson, L. (1993). *Down on their luck: A study of homeless street people.* Berkeley and Los Angeles: University of California Press.

Snow, D. A., Anderson, L., Quist, T., & Cress, D. (1996). Material survival strategies on the street: Homeless people as *bricoleurs.* In J. Baumohl (Ed.), *Homelessness in America* (pp. 86-96). Phoenix, AZ: Oryx Press.

Solomon, C., & Jackson-Jobe, E (Eds.). (1992). *Helping homeless people: Unique challenges & solutions* (pp. 15-28). Alexandria, VA: American Association for Counseling and Development.

Sommer, H. (2000). *Homelessness in urban America: A review of the literature.* Conference on Urban Homelessness and Public Policy Solutions. Berkeley, CA: Institute of Government Studies Press, University of California at Berkeley. Retrieved April 27, 2010, from http://igs.berkeley.edu/events/homeless/NewHomelessnessBook1.pdf

Springer, S. (2000). Homelessness: A proposal for a global definition and classification. *Habitat International, 24*(4), 475-484.

Sullivan, M. A. (1991). The homeless older woman in context: alienation, cutoff, and reconnection. *Journal of Women and Aging, 3,* 3-24.

Susser, E., Streuning, E. L., & Conover, S. (1989). Psychiatric problems in homeless men. *Archives of General Psychiatry, 46,* 784-859.

Susser, I. (1996). The construction of poverty and homelessness in U.S. cities. *Annual Review of Anthropology, 25,* 411-435.

The Urban Institute. (2000). *A new look at homelessness in America.* Washington, DC: author.

Toro, E A., & Warren, M. G. (1999). Homelessness in the United States: Policy considerations. *Journal of Community Psychology, 27,* 119-136.

Torquati, J. C. (2002). Personal and social resources as predictors of parenting in homeless families. *Journal of Family Issues, 23(4),* 463-485.

12 ways libraries are good for the country. (1995, December). *American Libraries, 26(11),* 1113-1119.

U. S. Conference of Mayors. (2003). Resolution No. 22. Endorsing 10 Year Planning Process to End Chronic Homelessness. 71st annual meeting, June 2003, Denver, CO.

United Nations Centre for Human Settlements (UNCHS). (2000). *Strategies to combat homelessness* (Series of Publications in Support of the Global Campaign for Secure Tenure No. 03/2000). Retrieved April 27, 2010, from http://ww2. unhabitat.org/programmes/housingpolicy/documents/HS-599x.pdf

Urban Institute. (1999). *Homeless programs and the people they serve.* Summary report of the national survey of homeless assistance providers and clients. Washington, DC: Urban Institute.

Weitzman, B. C. (1989). Pregnancy and childbirth: Risk factors for homelessness? *Family Planning Perspectives, 21(4),* 175-178.

Winkleby, M. A., & Fleshin, D. (1993). Physical, addictive, and psychiatric disorders among homeless veterans and non-veterans. *Public Health Reports, 108(1),* 30-37.

Wong, Y. I. (1997). Patterns of homelessness: A review of longitudinal studies. In D. R Culhane & S. R Homburg (Eds.), *Understanding homelessness: New policy and research perspectives* (pp. 135-164). Washington, DC: Fannie Mae Foundation.

Wong, Y. I., & Piliavin, I. (2001). Stressors, resources and distress among homeless persons: A longitudinal analysis. *Social Science and Medicine, 52,* 1029-1042.

Zatakia, J., Toro, E A., Tompsett, C., & Guzicki, M. (2002, November). *Predictors of public opinion on homelessness: Results from two national surveys.* Paper presented at the annual meeting of the American Public Health Association, Philadephia.

WEBOGRAPHY

The following is a selected list of websites of organizations in South Florida that address homeless needs.

Camillus House
http://www.camillus.org

Community Health of South Florida
http://www.chisouthfl.org

Community Parternships for the Homeless
http://www.cphi.org

First United Methodist Church
http://www.fumcmiami.com

Florida Immigrant Advocacy Center
http://www.fiacfla.org

Goodwill Industries of South Florida
www.goodwillsouthflorida.org

HOPE in Miami Beach
http://www.hopeinmiamibeach.org

Legal Services of Greater Miami
http://www.lsgmi.org

Miami Bridge Youth & Family Services
http://www.miamibridge.org

Miami Rescue Mission
http://www.miamirescuemission.com

Salvation Army
http://www.salvationarmy.org

St. Joseph's Church
http://www.stjosephmiamibeach.com

St. Patrick Church
http://www.stpatrickmiamibeach.com

St. Vincent De Paul Thrift Store
http://www.svdpusa.org

StandUp For Kids
http://www.standupforkids.org

Temple Beth Sholom
http://www.tbsmb.org

This book is typeset in Goudy Old Style.
A classic typeface originally created by Frederic W. Goudy
for the American Type Founders in 1915, Goudy Old Style
is considered to be among the most legible and readble serif
typefaces for use in print. The italicized version of Goudy Old
Style was designed by Frederic W. Goudy in 1918.

www.ingramcontent.com/pod-product-compliance
Lightning Source LLC
Chambersburg PA
CBHW072123020426
42334CB00018B/1692